OVERCOMING MEDIOCRITY

To Jacqueline

Hugs +
Success!

Jackie

RESILIENT WOMEN
OVERCOMING
Mediocrity©

A unique collection of stories from resilient women who have created their own lives of significance!

Presented by Christie L. Ruffino

DPWN Publishing

www.DPWNpublishing.com

Copyright © 2017 by Dynamic Professional Women's Network, Inc.

All rights reserved. No portion of this book may be reproduced by mechanical, photographic or electronic process, nor may it be stored in a retrieval system, transmitted in any form or otherwise be copied for public use or private use without written permission of the copyright owner.

This book is a compilation of stories from numerous experts who have each contributed a chapter. It is designed to provide information and inspiration to our readers.

It is sold with the understanding that the publisher and the individual authors are not engaged in the rendering of psychological, legal, accounting or other professional advice. The content and views in each chapter are the sole expression and opinion of its author and not necessarily the views of DPWN Publishing, Christie Lee Ruffino or the Dynamic Professional Women's Network, Inc.

For more information, contact:
DPWN Publishing
A division of the Dynamic Professional Women's Network, Inc.
1879 N. Neltnor Blvd. #316, West Chicago, IL 60185
www.dpwnpublishing.com
www.ourdpwn.com

Printed in the United States of America

ISBN: 978-1-939794-11-6

Dedication

To every woman who does not believe she can make a difference and to every woman who believes she can move a mountain.

To every woman who continually makes sacrifices for those she loves and to every woman who prioritizes those moments when she can pamper and take care of her own needs.

To every woman who believes that she should settle for the life she has and to every woman who has overcome great odds to create her own life of significance.

To the resilient women in this book who have shared their stories with you in hopes that their lessons of pain will become your lessons of power.

To the women in my life who believe I am significant and whom I believe are priceless.

The Power of a Story

There is nothing more important in this world than the relationships we build and the legacy we leave in the lives of those who have crossed paths with us on our journey of life. It's the experiences we have along this journey that define our individual uniqueness and create our own powerful personal blueprint or our unique story snowflake.

It is this blueprint that can empower us to possess a distinct advantage over every other person in this world if leveraged correctly and shared. If we don't have the courage to share our snowflake, it will be lost forever. No one will have the same story and no one can repeat your story. Therefore, those who come after you will never learn anything from what you experienced and what you learned.

I feel that the most significant thing we can do to add value back into this world is to master the narrative of our lives. All of our leadership and moneymaking abilities rest in our ability to discover, craft and deliver our personal story or message in a way that will allow people to connect to us. The right story shared at the right time with the right person can alter the trajectory of their life.

We also have the ability to learn from other people's stories and change the direction of the stories we are living to shape our ultimate destinies.

Power to you and the story of your life!

Success cannot be obtained by merely doing what is required, but by doing what you need to do, against all odds, at a level of excellence above all others.

— Author Unknown

Introduction

Welcome to our fifth *Overcoming Mediocrity* book featuring an amazing lineup of resilient women. The stories in this book are about strength, faith, and courage. They are about having the confidence to believe in ourselves, even when those we love don't. They are about having the courage to do things that are hard, even when we may not want to. And they are about remaining resilient through all of life's ups and downs because that is what, as women, we do brilliantly.

It is easy to become complacent and live a mediocre life, but these women made a choice to live lives of significance and share them with you throughout the pages of this book.

Our first book, *Overcoming Mediocrity—Dynamic Edition,* was a smashing success! It was released in May 2013 with 22 participating authors sharing their stories to inspire other women to overcome and succeed. That book became the #1 downloaded Kindle book on the very first day of its release, in the motivational genre category, allowing the authors to claim the distinguished Amazon Bestselling Author status. It was so exciting!

My initial goal with this project was to create one collaborative book, collecting incredible stories from women I admired who were friends and members of the Dynamic Professional Women's Network (DPWN). I knew how transformational an experience like this had been for me when I was asked to share my story in a similar book compiled by a mentor of mine, Michelle Prince. I also knew how having a book to share in the business community gave me additional credibility and exposure. What I didn't know was how transformational the stories would be for the readers who related with one or more of the women inside that first book. Those blessings would come later.

I had built a thriving business providing women a successful system to build a strong referral network as a DPWN member, so it was a logical transition to also provide them a platform to share their "Super Heroine" stories. This would allow them the opportunity to leverage "Author" status and gain additional exposure and credibility for their business. It would also enable them to receive greater blessings as they collaborated with other authors and shared their stories with a wider audience. These books have taken on lives of their own and have made a greater impact than ever anticipated. It is exciting to read testimonials from women who have read one of the books and connected with the inspirational stories inside. It is even more exciting when one of them decides to share their story in one of our future books.

Because of the overwhelming success of that first book, we produced a second book, *Overcoming Mediocrity—Courageous Women* that launched in April 2014, then the *Strong Women* edition released in May 2015 and finally the *Remarkable Women* edition released in November 2016. Each of these books hit #1 on Amazon in multiple categories also awarding them the distinguished Amazon Bestselling Author status.

It is with great honor and pride that I am able to share with you stories from the resilient women on the following pages of the fifth anthology in this series. I have had the pleasure of getting to know each of these ladies and learn a little about the stories they planned to share. I'm deeply inspired by the courage they're exhibiting for sharing the personal details of their lives with the sole intention of allowing the reader to learn from their experiences and to possibly spare themselves a little pain. This demonstrates courage and strength, as well as the humility and heart of a true go-giver. These women, while still on the amazing journey of their lives, all have great things yet to come. They are women who you should know, learn from and emulate.

This book is about not only encouraging you to become and remain resilient, but awakening you to recognizing the true value of collaboration. The women in this book wanted to make the biggest impact on the world by sharing their stories in a book that would get massive exposure in an attempt to transform as many lives as possible. They could have kept their stories private. That would have been the safest and easiest path for them. But they made a decision to step out of their comfort zone and share the narrative of their lives with you.

I am blessed to have the opportunity to share this book with you. I hope you feel as blessed to receive the value these women and their stories offer you.

Hugs & Blessings,

Christie

Table of Contents

Monique Hicks: Failure Is Not an Option.. 1

Angie Engstrom: Getting Yourself Unstuck 11

Misty Totzke: From Trainwreck to Triumph...................................23

Sharan Tash: Chubby Child to Healthy Senior:
    a Trilogy to Health 35

Melissa Laverty: The Life Cycle of Business 45

Jackie Simmons: No Place Left to Hide 53

Nancy Abramovitz: Side Dishes 63

Ylona Cavalier: RISE & SHINE —
    The Good Lord Is Upon Us!..75

Dorci Hill: It Takes Guts to Find Your Glory 83

Marci D. Toler: Lead Strong, Serve Selflessly,
    Be Your Best Self and Love Well — Lessons from Iraq 91

Irina Zlatogorova: Three Life Lessons...99

Svietlana Lavrentidi: It Was All Worth It.....................................107

Michele Riley Swiderski: Navigating
    Life Part Two...Let It Go 115

La Tanya D. Hinton: When the Smoke Clears...............................123

Danielle Di Cosola: My Rock Bottom Blessing 131

Jennifer Pestikas: Keep Moving Forward.....................................139

Kathy Rosner: Great Things Happen
    Outside of Your Comfort Zone 147

Michelle L. Sutter: Recalculating: Life's GPS 157

Sherry E.T. Rauch-Dehbozorgi: Never Take a NO from
    Someone Who Was Never Empowered to Give You a
    YES in the First Place...167

Jennifer Truesdale: Brittle, Not Broken 175

Jeanmarie Dwyer-Wrigley: Unlikely Angel.......................181

Monique Hicks

Failure Is Not an Option

I decided that I wanted to be different. I came from a broken marriage, the product of an addict father and a single mother. I definitely knew what I did not want to be, but I didn't quite know what I could be. Regardless of their own interpersonal struggles, my mom and dad both had many talents and skills. Genetically, I was half of each and knew I was capable of all of their good and bad. However, I learned early on about choices and decided I was going to try to choose wisely. I was smart and driven; always the girl raising her hand to answer every question in class. I had a thirst for knowledge. It never fazed me when people called me names for being the teacher's pet or when they didn't pick me first for kickball. This is where I learned that the cheese stands alone. In high school, I fit in and was in many social groups. However, I was a round peg in a square hole. I hoped that there was something more and something bigger. I looked for a way out into the world by taking my SATs early and applying to college in the eleventh grade. To my great surprise, I was accepted into the University of Miami's early admissions program. I never even told my friends or family that I was applying. I never thought I would get in and I applied to only one school because that's all the money I had. So, I guess you could say I got the golden ticket. With little hesitation, I told my family and friends and prepared to leave for university at the end of my junior year.

Miami was fun, but it was a little more freedom than I was prepared to handle at seventeen. I wasn't prepared to be an adult. I wasn't prepared for three hundred and fifty kids in my biochemistry class with a Russian professor I couldn't understand and no one to help me. I doubted my abilities and myself and didn't know where to turn to for help. I was humbled and taken aback by the world I so strongly wanted to be a part of. I saw many things I had never seen before and, frankly, I was completely overwhelmed for the first time in my life. During this time, my father also passed away unexpectedly. This took a toll on our entire family. Because I was of age and my parents were divorced, I was legally responsible for his end of life decisions. I can't describe looking into my grandmother's eyes and knowing that we had to let her son go. It's not supposed to be that way, and a parent should never have to bury their child. Combined with this devastating loss on so many levels and my self-doubt at school, I needed to check out and re-balance myself.

I took a few years off and worked in the restaurant industry. I quickly grew into a management role at any place I worked. I was soon recruited into fine dining. The restaurant industry is where I learned the art of customer service and thinking quickly on my toes to solve problems with a smile. I made good money and learned to be a connoisseur of some of the finer things in life. However, I still wanted more. I wanted stability and security. I wanted to make sure I never went hungry or was scared about making rent. This is when I decided that nursing school would ensure my security. I enrolled and began taking my pre-requisites. Studying and memorizing everything after being out of school for several years was really hard work. I wanted to get done as quickly as possible because I was paying for my own education and taking three science courses per semester. I applied to nursing school and was admitted. I was a sponge. I hardly had to study for tests because I was so enthralled with this education that all I could do was think and talk about medicine and the human body. After graduation, I applied to a hospital and worked for a few years in Emergency and Mother-/Baby Medicine. I loved every second of my new career and this is where I learned of my love of helping people.

However, the bug was itching again for me to get my bachelor's degree and further my education. I thought about medical school and decided on a pre-med track. I ended up graduating with an interdisciplinary degree and majors in physics and humanities with a minor in health. After deciding I would attempt medical school, I flew out to California to attend a medical school symposium with over seventy schools looking for prospects. I ended up meeting a Navy dentist who was recruiting for the military. We spoke about the military and the possibility of them paying for my medical school, which seemed very appealing. He told me about a humanitarian mission called Continuing Promise that he was preparing to leave for in a month or so. We talked and it just so happened they had a shortage of nurses for this mission. I asked if they would allow a civilian, thinking this might be the perfect opportunity to see if the military could be a fit for me. He made a few calls and I was accepted to be a part of the mission. Without hesitation I told my employer and my roommates that I would be going on a four-month journey on the USNS Comfort. I had a garage sale and sold everything I owned to pay for my car, insurance and bills while I was gone. I parked my car in my mom's garage and set off on the journey of a lifetime. We traveled to Haiti, Dominican Republic, Antigua, Barbuda, Nicaragua, El Salvador, Colombia and Panama. I went through the Panama Canal and crossed the Equator twice! I became an honorary Shellback, a term given to members of the Navy who cross the Equator after you complete a series of fun events and challenges, which may or may not be a form of hazing, but it was all in good fun. We provided medical and surgical care for citizens of these countries during our visits. I learned about the people, their countries and their challenges with healthcare and basic human rights. This was an incredible eye-opening journey that gave me a true passion for helping others. It was an experience and a journey I will never forget and always hold true to my heart.

When I returned home from the ship, we were in the height of the financial recession and the hospitals were in a hiring freeze. The whole reason I chose nursing was because I was told a nurse could always get a good job. I then applied at a local company in a plastic surgeon's office. I was hired and trained to run the medical weight loss portion of the practice. This is where I learned to manage people—both staff and clients—and help people to both set and reach their goals. This was an incredible learning opportunity that taught me how people operate and how to help them establish discipline. I found patterns and devised methods to help them overcome setbacks while still cheering them to success. This was because I was regularly hearing very similar stories of women and men putting themselves last and putting their careers, children, partners or homes first. I realized this was a common theme. However, for the people who decided to make a change and started putting themselves first, I saw tremendous positive outcomes. I became dedicated to helping them through their journey. I listened, learned and then applied my principles of success. It really worked. After a few successful years, I decided it might be time to start my own business. My sister had recently moved to Atlanta, and I decided to move there as well and give it a try. Over several months, I had saved up ten thousand dollars and knew I would need every penny for my journey to become an entrepreneur.

At twenty-six, I moved in with my little sister, rent-free, and began the process of searching for the first location for my new business, Vitality Med Spa. I had no business plan. But I had determination, a strong work ethic and just enough naive youth to perpetuate my plan. I searched vigilantly every day. Atlanta is a very large city with many different pockets and I visited every single one searching for the right location. But every time I found a great property, it was so far out of my budget that I would blow through my savings for just the first month's rent and security deposit. I went to a few banks for a loan but every single one said, "No, come back when you have three months of revenue." I thought that surely defeated the process of a start-up loan. So, I decided to try the suburbs, and to my surprise, I found a great location. On that day, I had no idea my life would change forever with one of those once in a lifetime chances. I still remember pulling up to the office and the dress I was wearing. I met the owner of the building, Clyde, and we immediately began an easy conversation about my dreams. He asked about me and he told me about his company. We began discussing the space for rent. He told me about the costs and it was in my budget. I had never done this before—with all the other places, we never made it past the initial costs before I figured out it wasn't going to work. He then asked me about the build-out needs of my space. He happened to be a contractor and started walking me through my plans. I knew what I needed in the space, but I never got to the build-out process. This is because I had assumed I would find an office much like you do an apartment. This is not usually the case. My heart sank. I knew I had underestimated. But then a miracle happened. He told me that he believed in me and saw something special. He said he was given a chance a long time ago and he wanted to do the same for me. He offered to build-out the 973 square foot space for me and only made me sign a year lease. This is when it all happened. In one short meeting, my life would never be the same. Within a few weeks, I was in my very first office. I filled it with my apartment furniture. It was shabby chic and very cute. I was the receptionist and the nurse and every other hat there was to wear. But I was happy. I was also scared, but I was so busy that I didn't have much time for doubts. I started putting my plan in place of what to do next.

It just so happened that I knew a family in the town where I opened my office and they helped spread the word. My friend, Kara, worked from home and came in to help me answer phones. We had a small group of clients that we had written down on a small note pad according to which day they started the program. They came in weekly for their weight loss check in. They received the best customer service ever. We were waiting on them, and if they didn't come in, we called them. We checked in and this made them feel important, so they kept coming back. This was the time to really make an impact, and we did. Within two months, I was able to cover all of the expenses besides payroll. I was living off my credit cards and Kara was pro bono. After four months, I was able to offer Kara a small stipend to come in regularly. After six months, I added more services to the roster including cosmetic injectables, aesthetics and cosmetic laser treatments. At nine months, I hired my first medical assistant, my medical director was coming in regularly and everything was falling into place. Twelve months into the practice, we were asked to participate in an event and offer our services at another business with similar clientele. We jumped at the offer and it was a huge success. There happened to be a vacant space a few doors down. I decided that was where my second location was going to be. I got down to business and negotiated my second lease. I paid for the build-out this time with profit. We opened on a Wednesday before Christmas and had a twelve thousand dollar opening week. I knew that weekend it was going to be a success. About six months later, I expanded my original location from 973 square feet to 2500 square feet. I also paid for this build-out with profit. Surprisingly, I tried to get a loan again, thinking about trying to keep working capital for business operations. However, although the business was doing very well, the banks still denied me because I hadn't been in business for three years. In hindsight, not taking any loans was the best obstacle I ever encountered. It made me work harder for what I wanted. It made me buy only what I could truly afford. And it all worked beautifully.

Growing up poor taught me to be resourceful and to be able to work with very little. It also taught me to make it the best I could. I learned the art of stretching a dollar from my mother. She worked three jobs and provided for my sister and me. She taught us the value of a dollar and the hard work required to make that dollar. Her expectations were always high, but I knew she never put anything in front of me that she wasn't willing to do herself. This is where I learned to be a strong leader and take no nonsense. It is also where I learned that failure wasn't an option. In 2016, after five years, fifteen employees, seventy service offerings and lots of entrepreneur education, it was time to move again as both of my leases were up. I decided to lease a 3500 square foot space in a bustling work, live and play area. The retail space was expensive, but I just knew if I built it, they would come. I self-financed the build-out with a well-negotiated tenant improvement allowance and a slew of business credit cards with zero percent interest for a year. By this time, I didn't even waste my time with the banks. I gave myself a year to pay it off and that's exactly what I set out to do. I decided to move both locations into this new, state-of-the art facility where we could focus on building the brand together.

Kara, my first pro bono employee, is now the general manager of Vitality

Med Spa and Plastic Surgery Center. I also employ a plastic surgeon, cosmetic surgeon, several nurses, laser technicians, estheticians and administrative talent. I don't like the word staff. I prefer talent, because that's what we are. We're talented professionals striving for the best medically based treatments for our clients' issues. As our constantly evolving industry grows, we want the best solutions. As industry leaders and pioneers, I decided we would offer a Center of Excellence to train other professionals in our industry. I've forged partnerships with our vendors to offer a Center of Excellence training facility for their devices as well. It's been an incredible journey so far. In five short years, I've built a company that is successful and changes the lives of the people who work for it and the people we proudly serve. I get the honor of telling my story and being considered a woman who has overcome mediocrity. I feel blessed to be part of something bigger, and humbled that I get to share it with others. My best advice would be to believe in yourself, trust your gut, surround yourself with people who inspire you to be better and work hard. Failure is not an option, because ultimately, there is no such thing.

Monique Hicks

Monique Hicks has been in the cosmetic and plastic surgery industry for over ten years. She has owned her own practice for over five years, specializing in the art of concierge medicine, talent development and business strategy. She has opened three practices offering over seventy different procedures and services. She works with multiple vendors and skin care companies to bring the best, most technologically advanced gold standards to her clients. She has a unique approach to working with people and strives to create true partnerships with people who believe in both her way of doing business and the products and services they represent. In addition to the companies she chooses to work with, she is just as selective of the people she chooses to surround herself with. Jim Rohn has said, "You are the average of the five people you spend the most time with." Monique loves hiring passionate, talented people who have a love for helping others and achieving their personal best. She truly feels this is the best combination and has managed to hire fifteen talented employees who seamlessly manage to shine in her leadership. In 2016, she was honored with the Pinnacle Award for the Best Female Small Business Owner of the Year.

Monique Hicks

Vitality Med Spa and Plastic Surgery Center

310 Town Center Ave., Suite A2

Suwanee, GA 30024

561-914-1444

mhicks@vitalitymedspamd.com

www.VitalityMedSpaMD.com

Angie Engstrom

Getting Yourself Unstuck

I am crying and shaken to the core. Relieved that we have a diagnosis but frightened at the new path we must navigate as a family. I am amazed at how one hour in a behavioral optometrist's office can rock my world.

An hour ago, I didn't even know what a behavioral optometrist was.

THE MESS

Life gets messy, both literally and figuratively.

When messes happen, how do you get yourself unstuck? How do you react, cope, and deal with circumstances beyond your control and move toward the life you desire?

I like the word "mess" because messes can be cleaned up. Reframing circumstances to the positive brings hope that allows me to see the possibilities rather than the obvious adversity in front of me. This belief was tested while raising our son. What follows is a brief overview of the journey that tested and strengthened me and my family, as well as some of the lessons learned along the way.

OBSERVING, QUESTIONING, AND COPING

Prior to this moment, my five-year-old son, Michael, was struggling socially, due to random behavior issues that no medical professional could explain.

Michael was an extremely happy, alert, and spirited toddler: imaginative, energetic, and adventurous. He was a constant ball of motion, and always kept us on our toes. But as his mom, I knew something was special about Michael.

By the time he was eighteen months old, I had heard many comments from people about how active he was. Therefore, I asked the pediatrician to rate his level of activity. After cautiously searching for the right words, the doctor finally looked directly at me and said, "You've got a livewire!"

What kind of diagnosis was that? However, if the doctor wasn't worried, why should I be?

In the controlled environment of our home, his behaviors were "normal." However, any time we were around other people, even family, he had unusual behavior outbursts that were loud, disruptive, and sometimes physical. As the mom, I felt the overwhelming blame—the mommy guilt—and thought, *Why can't I control my child's behavior?* I observed closely, looking for any pattern that triggered his outbursts, but no such pattern emerged. His unusual behaviors were completely random. Yet the shame of this behavioral mess constantly overshadowed my spirit. Seeking peace amidst this "noise" became my daily survival tactic in order to keep my sanity.

Think of his behavior like a clock—tic tock, tic tock, tic tock, CLUNK! tic tock, tic tock, CLUNK! He seemed like a normal kid; and then out of the blue, with no warning, and no way to predict it, he would have a behavior outburst—the CLUNK!—so obnoxious that everyone would stop, look with amazement, and not know how to react. People would scatter as if saying, "Excuse us. We'll find other kids to play with." Social isolation became the new norm for our family.

Going anywhere in public, especially out to restaurants and shopping, were projects that needed strategic planning and a mental helmet to protect my sanity, as I learned to dodge judgmental stares.

Have you ever seen a mom trying to control a sensory overloaded kid: loud, impulsive, can't sit still, and needs constant prompting to stay on task?

Hello. Nice to meet you.

Preschool was the tipping point for me. The school would frequently call me to pick up Michael early because he was so disruptive. On the days he did make it the whole two hours, it became the norm for all the other kids to run up to me like it was a competition to tell me all the bad things he did that day. My heart ripped open every day I had to endure the judgement, even from children. Picking him up from school was the lowest point of my daily existence.

Something was very wrong. The behaviors that the teachers and kids were describing were not anything I had ever witnessed when he was in my care. It was as if they were describing a completely different kid.

With kindergarten around the corner, I knew we needed more time to figure out the best place for Michael socially and academically.

THE HIDDEN OBSTACLE REVEALED

This is when I found myself in a behavioral optometry office.

Behavioral optometry is an expanded area of optometric practice that takes a holistic approach to eye and vision care, not just focal vision. I was introduced to new terminology such as: ambient vision, convergence insufficiency, saccadic deficiency, occupational therapy, sensory processing disorder, vestibular, and proprioception. All these new labels and terms.

What just happened to my world?

Did you know that a comprehensive eye assessment is recommended for infants during their first year of life? As a new mom, I wish I'd known that. I was mistakenly led to believe that I could wait until school age to have Michael's eyes checked. Babies obviously can't read, so what are the doctors looking for? If eye and vision issues are diagnosed and treated early enough, many problems can be avoided, including learning and permanent vision impairment. One in every ten children is at risk for undiagnosed eye and vision problems. Who knew, right? Check out www.InfantSEE.org if you know anyone under the age of one. That tidbit of prevention could possibly save a family a lot of grief.

This certainly was a mess for our family, while at the same time a relief since we finally had a medical professional explain a hidden obstacle causing Michael's behavior issues after five years of observing, questioning, and coping the best we could.

After only fifteen minutes in her optometrist chair, the doctor faxed a prescription to a rehabilitation hospital for an occupational therapy evaluation, put therapeutic glasses on my five-year-old son, and sent us out the door with pamphlets and homework.

Just four months earlier, we were at the pediatrician's office with a clean bill of health. Now, we were being sent to a rehabilitation hospital.

Talk about a SHOCK!

THE CIRCUMSTANCES

This news was an answer to our prayers for clarity, but the plan and path laid before us was a very costly one, on all levels, including financially, emotionally, and relationally.

Our family was at a crossroads. Was this the path to take, and how do we redesign our lives to make it happen?

Many questions and conversations occurred while navigating the proper, successful path to stability. All the individuals involved needed to agree with the plan in order to make consistent progress. Disagreement and resistance to new ideas slowed the process down.

The objections and excuses could have taken over and kept us from moving forward. Here is a partial list:

"That program is too expensive."

"I'm not paying out of pocket for that treatment. If insurance doesn't cover it, forget it."

"That's too far to drive. Too much time and gas money."

"We need another opinion."

"You know how much time I will have to take off work? We can't afford that."

Dwelling on the mess wasn't going to help anyone. Focusing on our family vision and creating a plan accordingly, despite the obvious obstacles, was essential. There were many excuses we could have made, but as a family, we allowed the big picture to drive our daily decisions.

COMMITTING TO THE PLAN

As CEOs of the household, my husband, Mike, and I defined everyone's roles. Mike took the financial burden, and I took the rest. I made the time to assemble the professional care team and drive the miles to get to everyone. My day became scheduled around our new priority: trusting this new treatment option for Michael.

Many miles, hours, and dollars later, the results of the treatments were slow and barely noticeable. So, the questioning continued:

"Are we doing the right thing?"

"Do we choose other options presented to us?"

"What other options do we have?"

Outside of the rehabilitation hospital, most of the people I talked to had never heard of sensory processing disorder (SPD). Others tried to give us labels that often overlapped with SPD. The pediatrician was not on board, so we were carving a non-traditional path for Michael's treatments that was not covered by insurance. We tried just about every known modality we could afford that aligned with our vision.

DOING WHATEVER IT TAKES

Homeschooling became the optimal choice because his behaviors were triggered any time people were around. The larger the crowd, the bigger the disruption. Public school was not a favorable option.

Our family business had residual money coming in which allowed me to be a stay-at-home working mom, but it wasn't enough to support this phase of our life.

LIFE SHATTERED

As the pressures mounted from decisions that needed to be made despite the unknowns, and disagreements and discussions along the way, it was easy to see how families break apart during these kinds of crises. Statistics show that families with kids that have special needs have a much higher divorce rate. Just knowing that statistic helped me decide not to become one.

It got to a point to where our funds were almost gone.

Eventually, my husband had had enough. "You are going to work and he's going to public school."

My world had now completely shattered.

Enrolling Michael in a public school knowing it was not the ideal environment for him elevated my prayer status into high gear.

For me, going to work meant starting a business, because that's what I knew how to do. What "job" was going to be flexible enough for our family's needs? If you can't find a way, make a way. So I created a business that worked within my schedule and gave me the flexibility I needed.

GETTING WORSE BEFORE GETTING BETTER

After entering public school, Michael gradually became a very troubled and unhappy kid. That environment magnified his learning disabilities and crushed his self-confidence. Something is definitely wrong when your fourth grader exits the school building and yells, "I'm done with this!" and intentionally runs into the path of a moving vehicle. I immediately contacted the school office to see what on earth happened that day. They said, "Oh, he had a great day."

How could this be happening! Back to the not knowing.

KIDS ARE LITTLE TEACHERS

Looking back on what I know now, that parking lot incident was Michael's way of telling the world, "I do not feel safe, I am broken, and I don't fit in here." He couldn't put it into words then, but as he got older, he voiced how broken he felt.

Heartbreaking.

Before entering school, Michael was happily living life following the peace in his heart. Sometimes I call this the still, small voice. But upon entering school and getting more input from others with more worldly experience than him, he began to doubt, question, and ignore that peaceful whisper in his heart.

FOLLOW PEACE

I was getting a lot of practice learning how to pay attention to the whispers in my heart that were gently urging me to make the tough decisions. However, to do that, I had to seek, with intentionality, the peace in my heart.

Peace became my new mentor.

Every decision seemed to come with an emotional charge. I was learning to stop feeding the voice that was trying to pull me down. I call this the "noise." I focused on feeding the voice that said, "Take this path," or "Make this choice," even when circumstances tried to steer me otherwise.

Here's what I mean by "follow peace."

Think of it as a knowing in your heart. Perhaps it is a whisper you hear in your heart that is not coming from your thinking. We heard it as a child when we were naturally excited about life. But as we grew and received input from others who had more confidence and experience than us, those voices started crowding this peaceful whisper to where perhaps we could no longer hear it or even knew it existed in the first place.

When we retrain ourselves to follow peace, a whole new way of life unfolds.

LET IT GO

I had to let go of the outcome and trust the processes the universe was providing.

After more advocating, Michael was transferred to a safer school environment.

At the same time, God led us to a fantastic program that ended up being the most intense. It incorporated every modality we were already doing independently plus more into one customized program. If you know of a child that struggles with any kind of behavioral or learning issues, please consider taking the initial assessment at BrainBalanceCenters.com. For Michael, they found a new hidden obstacle: brain hemispheric imbalance.

However, this modality was the costliest of all the treatments we had ever considered. Once again, do we make this investment in finances, time, and miles? This miraculous solution would not have presented itself if it wasn't meant for us. Our job was to step out in faith. We did, and it proved to be the missing piece we needed to assist Michael to the next level of stability.

I'm all about getting to the root of an issue so that the results are lasting. If you think like me, at the very least, invest in the evaluation portion; and then make a quality decision from the data they uncover for you.

PRESENT MOMENT

This story only illustrates a fraction of the drama it took to help our son. I am happy to report that Michael is in a stable place; and it was worth every tear, tough conversation, and mile driven.

We have our happy kid back and peace rules at the heart of our family. The past is done, the future is bright, and we find the joy in each moment with the experiential knowledge that wholeness always was, and always will be, with us when we live daily from this place of flow and ease.

HERE'S WHAT MOST PEOPLE MISS

After years of sitting in waiting rooms, I met a lot of families. I love observing people. It was very clear to see the difference between the parents with a confident presence and peaceful demeanor, and those who couldn't quiet the noise to set their priorities and make decisions.

When you find your peace, you find your power.

Messes happen, and how we act and react to the messes directly affects the outcome. We can choose our attitudes, our actions, and our association. Those daily choices make all the difference as we get ourselves unstuck and move toward the life we desire.

If we keep getting tripped up by our messes, it slows us down and can derail us from reaching the target. Some people don't even know their target. Be deliberate about the life you want to create. Vision creates the energy that you need to take the next step. Allow that energy to drive you through the mess toward creating the newest version of the masterpiece of your life.

I encourage you to cast a clear vision for your family based on your values, create a plan, and be accountable to the small, daily actions of that plan as you follow peace along the way. Know that the noise will come, but allow your family's vision to guide each decision. When the plan gets challenged -- and it will -- decide to live moment by moment by following the small whispers in your heart.

IN CLOSING

When life gets messy, how do you pick up the pieces and craft the next layer of your masterpiece called life while keeping your sanity intact? How do you get yourself unstuck from the messes of life?

Looking back, I see how this experience has strengthened me for my mission in life. I now coach families and entrepreneurs on how to focus their time to achieve more in their day, while making plenty of time for their family's needs.

There is greatness inside you. You will either impact this world in a positive way or allow the external circumstances of life to keep you down. Don't leave it up to chance. Choose to live despite the circumstances and make an impact on others that will last beyond your lifetime. It's up to you to stay in charge of your daily attitudes and decisions, and it's worth every effort necessary to move toward this new lifestyle of living.

Through lessons learned from this story and many others, the Achieve More coaching, seminars, and workshops were developed. You can learn more at www.GettingYourselfUnstuck.com, including a free download to get you started. If you resonated with this message, I'd be honored to connect with you.

The power is in you. Life is too precious to waste another moment being stuck. Break through your obstacles, create the processes and systems you need, and to move with intention toward the life you want.

FOLLOW PEACE

Angie Engstrom

Author / Professional Keynote Speaker / Life Design Expert / Entrepreneur

Angie brings simplicity to the complex issues of business and personal life. There is an unshakable mission in Angie's soul to instigate change, empower, and impact others to achieve more in less time so that they can live their life on purpose and achieve their dreams.

Angie is the founder and facilitator of the weekly talk show Productivity Conversations, where listeners call in to ask about improving their productivity, organization, and any blocks around achievement in business and life. Using her skills as an active improvisation artist at Second City Chicago, she illuminates a unique perspective on whatever "mess" you may be dealing with. One of Angie's mottos: if you can't find the fun in your business, you are doing something wrong.

She is the author of two books, *Getting Yourself Unstuck* and *Overcoming*

Mediocrity. She is also the creator of the Achieving More business seminars, workshops and coaching programs.

Angie lives in Downers Grove, Illinois with her husband, Mike, son, Michael, and schnauzer, Austin. She is known in her community as Awesome Angie because she honors the awesomeness in you.

Angie Engstrom
Getting Yourself Unstuck
Downers Grove, IL 60516
630-909-3867
angie@angieengstrom.com
www.AngieEngstrom.com
www.GettingYourselfUnstuck.com
www.LifeDesignExpert.com

Misty Totzke

From Trainwreck to Triumph

To be resilient means the ability to recover quickly from difficulties. Resilience. It sounds like such a strong, powerful word, doesn't it? The way it rolls off your tongue, the way you sit up just a little straighter when you say it and the feeling of boldness it puts in your chest. It is the way you can look at your past with that "holy crap, I don't know how I made it out of those fires alive, but I did!" feeling.

Maybe if you are like me, years ago, though, hearing the word resilience makes you shrink back and feel small, like you're under a dark raincloud, the feeling of "life's happening to me and I'm just trying to survive." If any of this resonates with you, I have good news. I have walked that walk for many years. I know that pain well and my hope is that my journey can help you choose to come out from underneath the darkness.

If this feels more like where you play, I'm about to tell you how I went from train wreck to triumph, all by finding the one thing that was missing all along—my true work and passion. They were things I had never thought to look for or even knew how to go about finding. Let me tell you how I found my purpose in the craziest journey and how it drastically altered the course of my life. My hope is that it might help you, the amazingly beautiful person reading this, to rise, stop conforming and realize that playing small in the world doesn't serve anyone. It is my intention for this story to inspire you to come out and play big in this magnificent world we have. There is a place for each of us here, if we only have the courage to peel back the layers, let our souls shine and light up the dark places for healing to happen.

I don't want to spend a lot of time in the past, but this book's theme is resilience—and I promised you a train wreck. Therefore, you do need to know pieces of where I've been to appreciate where I'm at now, where I'm headed and the things I've been able to survive and rise from. My journey to find myself and my true work started unintentionally. I was a college grad with a shiny new business administration degree that I didn't have the slightest clue what to do with. I knew I had a burning passion to work with animals, specifically in animal welfare. However, any job I would have wanted was far away from my Illinois home. I had just moved back to Illinois from being away in Arizona attending college, so relocating again was out of the question for a number of reasons. Most prominent of those reasons was my mother, who had been sick with cancer, a number of inflammatory diseases and life-altering side effects since I was fourteen years old. By the time I graduated college, her illnesses were a way of life for my family and me. Learning to be a caretaker at such a young age takes its toll on the mind and body, and trying to ignore the lurking emotional baggage inside of me from "life happening to me" was incredibly painful.

As soon as I moved home, I went to work for my dad, who owned an intermodal repair company. Since I had a business degree and he owned a business, it was a good fit, especially since I had no idea what else I was going to do. I worked there for about six years before coming to the realization that though I loved getting to see my family every day, the job was very unfulfilling. While it was very demanding, it taught me a lot about time management and how to juggle wearing multiple hats in the same day. At that point, I had quite a bit of heaviness on my shoulders—mom was still sick and required time and energy from everyone around her, the job I had just didn't do it for me and I didn't feel like I was really going anywhere. I just felt stuck in a perpetual Groundhog Day.

If you're asking yourself why I stayed working there, I have a good reason. I grew up watching my mother work anywhere from two to three jobs to support our family. Most of my childhood was spent with my mom raising me herself along with my dad and extended family who lived with us on and off all throughout my childhood. It's evident that it really did take a village to raise me. I grew up seeing a woman care for her family while doing what she needed to do to survive, provide and sneak in her own joy here and there. For me, growing up watching this, I really didn't know what I didn't know. Not only did I not know how to intentionally seek out experiences or work that filled me with fulfillment and happiness, I really didn't how to go about finding and connecting with my authentic self to honor what I had been given life to do here.

In 2013, I accidentally found essential oils. I say accidentally because I wasn't actually looking to find what I found. Times were tough financially and I was looking to make my own cleaning products. Thanks to Pinterest, I found many recipes that used essential oils. After some research and experience with lesser quality oils, I stumbled across doTERRA. I had no idea about the journey I was about to embark on. In no time I was using oils for all sorts of different things. I was making my own products, but the physical and emotional support I was finding from oils was incredible. I then found out you could actually create a sizeable income for yourself by educating others about these oils. I welcomed any extra income and soon dove straight into building my own essential oil business. This was the trailhead of my transformation.

Prior to being introduced to essential oils, living life a little bit more natural-minded wasn't completely new to me. When I moved home from Arizona, I decided to become a vegetarian, based on my beliefs about animal welfare and cruelty. Since I knew my heart hurt for animals, I decided to take some courses at the Humane Society University for the future when I would somehow be able to make animal welfare into a career. Learning more about conventional farming put more nails in the coffin on my past carnivorous eating habits. Being a vegetarian, while a great idea, was hard work for me. I was constantly on the go, already working one full-time job and embarking on building another business. Since I had not yet been introduced to the idea of meal prepping, I relied heavily on processed packaged food, bread products, veggies and rice.

About a year after becoming a vegetarian, I started to notice that I was getting these red, flaky patches on my face. A couple of trips to my dermatologist, some blood tests and biopsies, and voila, I had myself a nice autoimmune disease. I was lucky that my case of lupus was just in my skin and was extremely mild. Thank God. I was fortunate that no medical intervention was necessary. However, I had no real clear reason why it was there. I knew autoimmune diseases were stress-related. At least, that's what they told me. I was working full time, building a side business, caretaking for a sick mom, financially strapped…yep, there was definitely an abundance of stress. That made sense. A year later, with the same lifestyle and food choices, I started noticing something wonky happening again. I was losing weight unintentionally. I was often anxious, dizzy and jittery. I talked very fast and I was exhausted all the time. After another trip to the doctor, I found out I had Grave's Disease, which is another autoimmune disease that is identified by a hyperactive thyroid. Because of the severity, quite a bit of medication was required to get me regulated, which took a couple years.

Because every piece of my story ties together, I need to mention that I grew up in a home where we relied heavily on medication. I really didn't know there were natural alternatives which could be used. When I discovered oils, a whole new world was unlocked for me. As the energetic clutter started to clear, I realized that there were many people using them. Many were health coaches, which I found both intriguing and mind blowing. I soon signed up to attend the Institute for Integrative Nutrition to become a health coach. It was there that I learned a ton about diet and lifestyle. It really forced me to take a good look at the food that I was putting into my body.

After a while, the word got out that I was not only teaching about essential oils, but I was also a health coach. I started getting connected to some really incredible people in the holistic community, including natural medicine doctors. They were more into figuring out the root cause of what was going on in the body instead of just treating the symptoms. Now, this was something I could get behind! After working with a few different practitioners, they all made the correlation that my body started breaking down when I took meat out of my diet. They basically told me that if I ever wanted to get better, I had to start eating meat again, even in minimal amounts.

Because I was a vegetarian based on ethics, I just couldn't wrap my brain around what felt like having to compromise my beliefs. There had to be another way. I continued to resist and decided to go to a different doctor. I hoped he would tell me something different. As luck would have it, he actually told me something worse. I found out that not only did my body thrive on animal protein, but I was sensitive to gluten, dairy and grains and I really shouldn't eat much soy. That's all I was eating as a vegetarian. It mirrored what I was taught in my health coaching classes—one person's food is another person's poison. All of the pieces came together and it hit me. I was literally making myself sick by what I was choosing to eat. When I ate gluten, grains and/or dairy, it weakened my immune system by causing the lining in my gut to leak (i.e., leaky gut). This caused my immune system to reflexively attack itself, resulting in my autoimmune diseases. I knew that I had to take gluten, grains and dairy out of my diet if I wanted to help my body and gut heal itself. Great, answers! But that would leave me with only fruit and veggies, how was that ever going to work?

Through all of this, I had to quickly learn how to honor my body. This included determining what it needed and what needed to be removed. Food was a big factor. Several stress factors also played a major role. Layer by layer, I started to cleanse the things I had control over. I had to first come to terms with being a conscious carnivore. I had to change what I was putting into my body, but I was not about to start putting in just anything. I compromised with myself. If I needed to put animal protein back into my diet to heal, I would at least try to put in grass fed, free range, non-GMO, hormone-free, etc. animal protein, whenever possible. Then I had to minimize or eliminate completely eating dairy, gluten and grains. Food issues—fixed.

I had overhauled all of my commercial products, such as haircare, skincare, shower items, etc. to essential oil infused products to take the place of crappy chemical alternatives. Luckily, I already had this covered. At this point, I had been using doTERRA's essential oils and products for about two years. I had overhauled all of my commercial products, such as haircare, skincare, shower items, to essential oil infused products to take the place of crappy chemical alternatives. I also had essential oils at my fingertips for literally anything that popped up in my house. The physical and emotional support from using them as a first defense was covered. The work I really needed to do here was making space and time for myself. Allowing myself to create stillness, sit quietly without distraction, pray, meditate, visualize and be in my own little world was always a challenge. In September 2016, I talked with my incredibly amazing energy healer friend, who told me I needed to turn back to my spirituality to help cope with many of the things that were headed my way. As luck would have it, I was introduced by a friend to an incredible group of women who made up an online, God-centered mentoring group called Big Life. Between Big Life, energy healing and a slew of really incredible books like HeatherAsh Amara's *Warrior Goddess Training,* the path back to my spirituality was paved in a way that was conducive to my lifestyle and beliefs. It was through these modalities that I learned how to surrender control, create space, raise my vibration, ask for help, learn how to pray and welcome in what was next in my path, with faith and love that there was a higher purpose for every single thing. Lifestyle issues—fixed.

Then there was the stress factor. When I thought of the things that really emotionally weighed on me every day, trying to cope with the rapid deterioration and imminent death of my mother was at the top of the list. We could stay here all day and talk about how remarkable and altogether heartbreaking my mother's health journey had been. With her bladder cancer diagnosis in 1998 and surrender to bone and lung cancer in 2016, she was sick for a total of about eighteen years straight. For more than half of my life, I'd witnessed what seemed like every possible medical condition, hospitalization, surgery, diagnosis, treatment, small bouts of remission and addiction a person can handle. She was a marvel at what the human body could tolerate. My mother's journey was an incredible gift. I was able to see firsthand what kind of life I didn't want. At thirty, my body was already giving me warning signs that I was veering onto a dangerous path. Noticing that my life oddly and unintentionally mirrored my mother's in many ways was enough to make me change my outlook on health and stress for good. Her death was the capstone on her suffering and the healing end she sought after for so long. It was also the start of deep healing for those of us who were left. One stress issue—fixed (though not in the way I ever intended).

The next big mountain was the frustration of still having to work my day job. I was way past my original exit date, due to many unforeseen detours and roadblocks. After my mom's death, things started shifting in my essential oil business. It was something that I attribute to her not wasting any time aligning things on the other side for me. People started to show up in my life, as if they were placed there purposely. As a result, new opportunities started to appear.

There was still the frustration which caused me to ask why things weren't aligning for me to leave. I asked, prayed, cried and begged. Finally, I got my answer. I absolutely love the oils as well as doTERRA's humanitarian mission to help heal the world by giving back and enriching lives in the sourcing countries. I loved being able to have simple solutions at my fingertips, like using peppermint to help energize me, citrus oils to lift my spirits on those really stressful days, a protective blend to help support my immune system and many other things. I realized, though, that I started making a business of it the moment I realized it was the way out of my job. I so badly wanted the time and financial freedoms to live my higher purposes of working in animal welfare, traveling and coaching. After connecting these dots, I realized that I had been building my business in survival mode because "life was happening to me and I was just trying to survive." It was hard and I struggled. I was never meant to leave my job that way. Now that I had done so much emotional cleansing and healing, I realized I had to start over. I wanted to create a business that not only aligned with my core values, but where I could really dig in and help better the lives of the people I got to work with. With 94% of people hating their jobs, I really sought to create a space where I showed up to be the lighthouse for someone else. This has been my path to walk so I could teach others how to do the same thing. I wanted to give others the opportunity to choose how to live their life.

Being introduced to doTERRA opened the door to finding my purpose and my true work. This has changed every piece of my life. It was the catalyst to me becoming a health coach, leader, mentor, healer, blogger, author, business owner, Warrior Goddess Facilitator, God-girl and someone who follows her own arrow and lives life big. It introduced and connected me to the most inspiring people who have supported and guided me through the toughest times I've seen. It's been my rock that's forced me to grow in the most expansive ways. I've learned to be incredibly intentional with my time and energy. I've learned to live with purpose, on purpose and with love every single day. I've learned to let joy lead and find the adventure in almost anything. I've learned how to emotionally cleanse through layers of emotional baggage, forgive myself and others and surrender to the flow of life. We never stop learning and growing. I am no different. I choose to welcome the lessons every day in an effort to never conform or live a mediocre life.

I've learned how to invite women who want to create a bigger life, filled with the things they love, to partner with me in doTERRA. Being able to watch someone else transform and fly like I have is a beautiful gift. Most of all, I've learned that you can live your life as a victim, as life is happening to you. This is what I did for most of my life. You can also choose to live in gratitude for the blessings and lessons that you get to learn. I now choose to be grateful for everything that happens. It doesn't matter whether it is amazing, good, bad or just plain ugly. At the time of this book, just five months after the loss of my mother, I'm plowing straight through one of the toughest life events a person can go through and instead of feeling like a victim, I'm feeling gratitude for everything it has taught me. Everything that happens is important for what it has to teach us, what it's cleansing, what it's aligning and what it's preparing us for.

My intention for you is to know that your mess is your message, and not giving up, figuring it out, is the most beautiful adventure that you'll ever go on. To find what really lights up your soul is very inspiring to everyone else around you, even if you don't realize it. *Your resilience comes from never giving up on yourself,* even when things seem hopeless. Figure out creative solutions, surrender to the flow of life and trust in divine timing, but do not ever give up. If you need some help, one of the most incredible books I ever read was HeatherAsh Amara's *Warrior Goddess Training.* I recommend it to everyone. I would love to hear how transformational it was for you.

I'll leave you with one of my favorite quotes that I was exposed to at the beginning of my journey. I love it very much and hope that you read it often:

"Our biggest fear is not that we are inadequate. Our deepest fear is that we are powerful beyond measure. It is our light, not our darkness, that most frightens us. We ask ourselves, 'Who am I to be brilliant, gorgeous, talented, fabulous?' Actually, who are you not to be? You are a child of God. Your playing small doesn't serve the world. There's nothing enlightened about shrinking so that other people won't feel insecure around you. You were born to make manifest the glory of God that is within you. It's not just in some of us, it's in everyone. And as we let our own light shine, we unconsciously give other people the permission to do the same. As we're liberated from our own fear, our presence automatically liberates others." —Marianne Williamson

Misty Totzke

Misty is a Certified Holistic Health and Lifestyle Coach, doTERRA Essential Oil Wellness Advocate and Humanitarian Entrepreneur. She has an insatiable zest for life, a clear vision of her true work in this world, incredible gratitude for her life's journey and born to find fun, joy and adventure in the simplest places. She has built her humanitarian-based business on the side for the last three years while working another full-time job, caretaking for her mother and thriving through autoimmune diseases. She calls the southern Chicago suburbs home, though her business allows her to serve needs anywhere in the world. Her inner light shines brightest for animal welfare and travel.

She holds a bachelor's degree in business administration from Arizona State University, a graduate certificate in animal advocacy and policy from the Humane Society University and her health coaching certification from the Institute for Integrative Nutrition. She is the visionary behind Squirrely Wanderlust Adventures, a movement to create adventure and exploration in your own local area. Misty is also personally trained by Heather Ash Amara as a Warrior Goddess Training Facilitator, which has added immense value to her leadership training with her doTERRA leadership team.

Misty's philanthropy includes being a member of the Junior League of Kane and DuPage Counties and Vice President of 100+ Women Who Care in Southern Will County.

Misty Totzke
630-387-9258
mistytotzke@gmail.com
www.mistytotzke.com

Sharan Tash

Chubby Child to Healthy Senior: A Trilogy to Health

Does size matter? It did for me—right from birth. I was a fat baby who grew into a chubby though active child, an overweight teen and an obese adult. But after a few aha moments that profoundly yet easily shifted my path, I'm now a fit, healthy senior who's also a certified fitness professional and founder of my own Skokie-based women's boutique fitness facility.

I was born fat. Not even plump, but downright fat. I looked like the Michelin Man from those vintage tire commercials, and my four outspoken siblings teased me incessantly about the resemblance. There were layers upon layers of fat on the arms, legs, stomach and neck of my baby body. I was oblivious at the time. But images of my fat baby self were captured and preserved for repeated family viewing by my dad, the film buff, who enthusiastically made that infamous home movie of me having my first bath. There I was, silently on display in black and white, squinting in the glare of the bright lights, way bigger than life size on the screen on those frequent family movie viewing nights. My siblings giggled and jeered unmercifully. There was my large tummy rising skyward, the visual that earned me the family nickname "Panza Ancha," meaning "wide belly."

Then came my first humiliation. It was my first encounter with a scale. I was unaware at the time, but mom's reaction was on film forever. When I was placed on the scale, the indicator went around a couple of times and there was Mom putting her hands over her face because she could not believe the number that was showing up. In later years, that movie brought a lot of noise from the peanut gallery and a lot of embarrassment to me. This continued throughout my childhood. I learned early on to expect and endure humiliation. But it never got easier or less hurtful.

Big Girl with Big Dreams

When I was three years old, I started dancing. I took tap, jazz and ballet. I continued the classes until I was eighteen, and even had dreams of becoming a dancer. However, during an audition, I was told that I would never make it as a professional because I was too big.

I loved dancing as a child and still do. But it, too, was not without its humiliation. Every year my dancing school had the students put on a recital for our parents and families. I don't remember if my brothers had to attend, but they did see my recitals, thanks to my dad and his trusty movie camera. My first recital was at Lane Tech High School. It was a tap routine to *Sweet Georgia Brown*. I was wearing a bright pink and turquoise costume with big dots on the very short skirt. My hat was pink and turquoise with big dots and stood straight up with a bow holding it under my chin. I wore bright red lipstick and my black patent leather tap shoes were shining brightly. The black ribbon that held my shoes on my feet was tied perfectly. I learned early on that everything had to be perfect.

My dad, of course, was filming the performance, and his big bright camera lights were staring me in the face. He was so proud of me and he told everyone around him, "There's my daughter—the little chunky one at the end." Yep. That was me—three years old and the little chunky one at the end.

The Body Size Roller Coaster

Growing up was painful. I was always hungry and ridiculed. I loved being active and got a lot of exercise, but I kept getting larger. I especially hated going shopping for clothes. My thin mom and slender sister would loudly roll their eyes every time I had to go to the next larger size in the "chubby girls" shop. It was during junior high school that I began trying diets.

Over the years, I tried every diet out there, ultimately with little success. I tried OptiFast—twice. I held out hope for this one since Oprah Winfrey had such luck with it. It was pure protein, with nothing but liquid protein all day. I attacked it eagerly, while also doing intensive weightlifting and daily aerobics. I lost thirty pounds in just ten days—success! However, I also ended up in the emergency room due to my body's reaction from carb deprivation. Undeterred, I went back to OptiFast for another week, lost another twenty pounds and had the same reaction. OptiFast, I concluded, was not for me, but I was still seeking that magic bullet. I turned to NutriSystem, Jenny Craig, Weight Watchers, the incredibly boring cabbage soup diet and the equally boring grapefruit diet, the Bead Diet, Physicians Weight Loss, Slim Fast, and Shakeology.

One day, I discovered Fen-Phen, which was a drug cocktail design to suppress the appetite. It worked and I was thrilled! It helped get my cravings down to where I was hardly eating anything again, but I was never sleeping either. I was getting about three hours of sleep at night. While others were sleeping, I was at the 24-hour fitness center working out at 1:00 AM and returning at 7:00 AM for another workout. But when the news came out about Fen-Phen being bad for the heart, I stopped using it. Not only did I promptly gain back all the weight I had lost on it, as an added bonus, I put on even more weight.

Along the way I got married—and divorced—four times. I eventually became the single parent of four children ranging in age from one to eleven. I always wanted to be a good role model for my children. I also knew that I'd want my children to get a college degree, but I had never finished mine. In order to make a better life for my children and me, I went back to college. I completed an undergraduate degree and graduated summa cum laude. I then went on for a master's in exercise physiology/cardiac rehab.

In addition to studying and child-rearing, I continued my exercise habit and was working out up to six hours each day. I enjoyed being active with my children. There I was, an active obese adult, coaching my children in swimming, football, soccer and baseball. Suddenly, in 1991, it hit me. I was at 357 pounds and on my way up to 400 pounds, when I realized that I was on a path of destruction. I knew that if I didn't make a change, I would surely die. The thought of not seeing my four children grow up and become parents, the possibility of not knowing my future grandchildren, made a huge impact on me. It woke me up and shook me up. I responded.

The Importance of Knowledge, The Magic of Mindset

At first, I took drastic measures that weren't healthy. I was eating only six hundred calories a day and not getting enough nutrients. I then started learning about the importance of eating more protein at all of my meals. In analyzing my eating habits, I realized how much I loved carbs and how much I was hooked on them. I was having carbs at every meal. At one point in my life, I could sit down at Burger King and eat two Whoppers with extra mayonnaise and onions, two large fries and a chocolate shake, and then take an order of fries to-go. Based on what I now know about the evils of carbs in fat production and fat storage, I knew my long romance with and dependence on carbs would have to come to an end. I embarked on a path of learning new ways of eating and shifting my attitudes and mindset away from my longtime addiction to and dependence on carbs. At the same time, I changed my way of exercising. I switched over to water exercises that were easier on my knees. After I lost 135 pounds and earned a National Academy of Sports Medicine personal training certification, I began my career as a personal trainer.

I began seeing a nutritionist who helped me identify my triggers and had me talk about why I wanted to eat the whole bowl of candy instead of just one or two pieces. I learned to use triggers to my advantage. I started eating a high protein diet that gave me energy throughout the day. I no longer eat packaged or processed foods. It's not a diet. It's an eating plan that I can maintain for the rest of my life.

Working on my nutrition led me to address my limiting beliefs in myself. Although my weight has gone up and down over the past twenty-five years, I am now in a place where I am healthier, happier, and in the best shape of my life. I have now reduced my weight—I no longer say "lost weight" because I do NOT want to find those pounds ever again!—by a total of 177 pounds and I'm continually reducing without deprivation.

My goal in becoming a personal trainer was to share my knowledge and experience with others who, like me, have struggled with size, weight, and the judgments of others. I tried to remain undaunted by the fact that my own body type was not that of the typical "size 0" fitness instructor. In 1992, I opened up a successful in-home personal training company that served Chicago's Orthodox Jewish community. My clients enjoyed the fact that I was "normal" size, but in great shape. I taught step class and high/low impact aerobics to clients and did one-on-one training.

A Fitness Vision

In 2001, I sold the business to one of my trainers and made a career change, entering the dental industry as a business trainer and consultant. But in 2013, my passions were pulling me back into fitness. I had been attending the weekly Zumba classes my daughter led, and my daughter often invited me to dance with her on stage.

One night after class, an offhand remark by a classmate—"Have you ever considered teaching Zumba?"—immediately resonated with me and profoundly changed my life. Cue the aha moment music and lights again. My longstanding vision of helping women of all sizes achieve health and fitness, and of inspiring them in some way through my example, came rushing to the fore. I sprang into action and, without stopping to consider its feasibility, I left my dental industry career and began to make my vision happen. Within six short weeks, I became a certified personal trainer through the National Academy of Sports Medicine, with advanced certification as a Women's Exercise Specialist and Senior Exercise Specialist. I also became a certified Bokwa Fitness instructor and a licensed Zumba instructor.

My vision of a fitness studio for women of all ages and sizes, large and small, began taking shape quickly. I took on substantial financial risk, most notably selling the home in which I had raised my children and investing all the proceeds into the venture. Despite challenges and setbacks, TASH (T-imeless A-geless S-izeless H-ealth) Wellness for Women is now an established, popular boutique-size facility in Skokie catering to women age 50+ who have fifty or more pounds to lose. TASH gets recognition in the local media and in the fitness community because our approach and philosophy are uncommon, if not unheard of, in the mainstream fitness industry. In a culture where youth, thinness, and small size are celebrated as the ideal and others are judged and made to feel scorned, TASH welcomes all women with encouragement and empathy. Customized exercise training, nutritional coaching, and an emphasis on accountability all help motivate our clients to achieve a healthier lifestyle.

I am proud of my certifications. I am certified by the National Academy of Sports Medicine as a personal trainer, and I'm a certified TRX Teams instructor—only one percent of all fitness trainers are certified in TRX. I also have specialized certifications in Senior Fitness and Women's Fitness and have taken advanced education in NASM's Behavior Change Specialist, Precision Nutrition, and Gray Institute's Functional Training. In addition, I'm a licensed Am I Hungry®? Mindful Eating facilitator.

Fitness: A New Paradigm

The weight loss industry has long been all about eat less and exercise more. Unfortunately, that model does not get into the real issues of weight management, which are mindset change, behavior change, sleep quality and quantity, and accountability. Those who use exercise alone to lose and maintain weight loss, after one year, showed a relapse of 99%. Those who use exercise and nutrition showed after one year a relapse of 90%. Those who used exercise, nutrition, and accountability showed after one year a relapse of only 11%. Add in the mindset, behavior change, and sleep and the numbers can only get better. However, those areas are the hardest for us to work on. Conventional programs do not address all six areas, but we do at TASH. Our members who are working on all six areas are having success, and they're changing their relationship with food and themselves. They have taken the emotion out of weight loss and food and they're in charge of their nutrition.

I am my client. I have walked in their shoes. I, too, tried every weight loss program and was unable to keep the weight off. Learning this new approach has allowed me to maintain my weight reduction while working on my mindset, which has and continues to be the hardest aspect of sustainable weight reduction. As a woman who fights the battle every day, I want to continue to be a role model for women who, like me, have tried multiple programs but were unable to maintain them. Deprivation is not the answer, and sustainable weight reduction and health are not just about "eat less and exercise more." My clients are proof of that. I want my clients to be healthy no matter their size or their age, and to find a lifestyle they can maintain without deprivation and self-sabotage. Health is more than a number on a scale or the result on a test. Health is an optimal quality of life.

I am a sixty-five-year-old, size 10–12 woman who has accepted that I will be this size for the rest of my life, as long as I exercise and eat properly. I have learned what works for me in the way of exercise and food. I want to be the role model for both adults and children who feel alone and who feel no one understands their weight issues. I hope to motivate individuals to want to attain a quality of life through lifestyle changes that they can maintain. I want to be an accountability partner for my clients. I want to help them succeed the way I have.

Learnings

My latest aha moment came in March 2016 during a continuing education program for my personal training certification. The instructor, someone whom I respect and have known for several years, was talking about the long stated fact that "a pound of fat is equal to thirty-five hundred calories." This so-called fact was debunked by a researcher. I bought the instructor's book, which led me to her Facebook page, which led me to three other doctors who had published research on obesity.

This latest discovery made me angry! I had learned and believed all I was told by the government, corporations, the food industry, and the fitness industry: "Eat less and exercise more," "Eat every two to three hours," "Eat forty to fifty percent carbs and cut back fat consumption." These oft-repeated tropes all turned out to be falsehoods perpetuated by those industries.

Through my own research, I have learned what works for me and what is working for my clients. I no longer take advice from anyone without delving into the money behind the research. If the author of a research article sits on the board or is paid by a corporation, that research has been tainted. I say this from personal experience, as I had put my trust in everything my professors said or my fitness magazines published.

No more! I've been having great results since March 2016 on my own journey to health. I have learned to apologize to my clients for continuing the rhetoric of false information and changing my views on the path to sustainable weight reduction. I try new paths first to test their viability before suggesting them to my clients. As I said, I am my client. I get it.

I have also learned that the anger I long harbored toward my mother for giving birth to a fat baby was unwarranted. My mother lost her father while she was pregnant with me. Due to that stress, her body released stress hormones to me in utero, which started my journey to insulin resistance before I was even born. Add to that equation the fact that I was given formula starting at two months and I was thus set up for obesity almost from birth. It was not my fault that I couldn't lose weight. I had poor information!

Finally, I have learned to be unafraid of saying, "I made a mistake."

The choices we make transform our lives…and can transform others as well.

Sharan Tash

Sharan Tash is the Founder of TASH Wellness for Women, a boutique facility in Skokie catering to women 50+ with 50-100+ pounds to reduce. A fitness professional who has struggled since birth with obesity, food cravings, and the judgments of others, Sharan understands what her clients are going through.

"Although I've been active my whole life, I've always been heavy. I was a large baby who looked like the Michelin Man. I was a fat teenager who became an obese adult. In 1990, I weighed 357 pounds and was well on my way to 400 pounds."

For Sharan, the aha moment occurred after she got off the diet merry-go-round and started working on her mindset. Her body image and food obsessions began to ease, and sustainable weight reduction took its place. Now age 65,

Sharan is a fit, healthy senior, and an inspiration to women of all ages.

Sharan wants women of all ages, sizes, and abilities to know that good health is more than numbers on a scale or on a test result! At TASH, the emphasis is on strength and health, not the scale. It's on exercising in a supportive, judgment-free environment and on nutrition coaching tailored to each woman's lifestyle.

Sharan Tash

TASH Wellness For Women

8816 Bronx Ave.

Skokie, IL 60077

847-379-5777

sharan@TASHFitness.com

www.TASHWellnessForWomen.com

Melissa Laverty

The Life Cycle of Business

Recently, I sat with a young couple who were embarking on a new adventure. The husband had been working for his father's business most of his life and was ready to break out on his own. He's a hardworking, charismatic electrician—the kind of guy who whistles while he works. She is a super-cute super-mom with a couple of little ones in tow. Together, they lead a full and busy life and were quite eager to take the leap into the world of self-employment. One day, she came to me in a bit of a panic: "I need to know everything there is to know about running a business before our first official day, which is in two weeks."

The first thing I had her do was take a couple of deep breaths. I then offered the following analogy: Starting a business is like having a baby. There is just no way to know everything about parenting the day you bring home that bundle of joy. Step one is simple. Don't kill the baby. Once you've got that down, you move on to figuring out how to get them to sleep through the night. Each day will bring new challenges and each baby is different. The same is true for owning your own business. Yes, there will be sleepless nights as well as frustrations and uncertainty. After all, you're creating a whole new entity, which is like bringing a new person into the world. However, with this new life comes endless possibilities. Putting things in this perspective seemed to help a lot. We set up an automated system to keep the books caught up and everything in check. As I write this, they are six months in and loving it. They've found their groove and are on track to double, and possibly triple, their income. Go team!

Relating to their struggles of balancing work and home life is easy for me. I've been both a single mother and a business owner for most of my adult life. I just love that my career allows me to help families like theirs discover and capture their dreams.

My journey to parenthood and business ownership were both unconventional. I hadn't really planned on either—they both just sort of happened. As a child, and through my years in high school, I worked hard to get good grades and do all that was expected of me. By all accounts, I was a nerd then and I still am now. Since there are all kinds of nerds, I'll clarify by saying I am a math nerd. I like things to be accurate and balanced. My two favorite classes in school were algebra and psychology. I didn't realize it then, but both would come in very handy.

By the time I finished my first year of college, I was exhausted. I had been working two jobs and squeezing a full course load into two days a week. Having no clue what I wanted to do with the rest of my life, taking some time off seemed like a good idea. So like any impulsive teenager would do, I dropped out of college and moved in with my new boyfriend. We were young and in love, or as the grownups call it, young and stupid. A few months later, I got pregnant. Although scientific studies have proven excessive marijuana use can lead to low sperm count, it is certainly not an effective form of birth control. Some things you just need to learn the hard way.

As you might imagine, this was not a planned pregnancy and was a bit of a surprise for my mother. When she heard the news, she started crying. I mean sobbing. This went on for weeks. She was a real hot mess. Two weeks into her pity party, I grabbed her by the shoulders, stared her in the face and said, "It's just a baby, Mom. I'm not sick, I'm not dying, I don't have AIDS and I'm not going to jail. It's just a baby." Back then, AIDS was a really scary thing, so that got her attention. I am not too sure if I shocked her out of it or if she simply dried up. Either way, the tears finally stopped. From then on, she was my rock. To be fair, I guess she always was my rock, but I hadn't figured that out yet. In fact, it took a few more years and a couple more life lessons before coming to the logical conclusion that my mother knows everything and is always right. As she had predicted, my baby's daddy was not up for the challenge and he ducked out of the parenting game after only a few months. I was twenty and on my own.

As any new parent would say, I had no idea what I was doing. The next few years were a blur. Luckily for me, I had been raised by a super hero who had trained me well. She taught me so much over the years; how to laugh when it hurts, how to stand up when I'm down and how to love every step of the way. She also taught me how to be thrifty and financially responsible. She's the queen of coupons and budgets. When it came time to do the grocery shopping and there was only twenty-three dollars left in my checking account, I made it happen. In fact, I had no clue how poor I was back then. I guess that was a benefit to having a child so young. I didn't realize I was making sacrifices because I'd never known any other way.

Admittedly, some days were harder than others. Whenever I would feel overwhelmed or feel like a kid trapped in an adult world, I'd give myself a time out. I would consciously stop whatever I was doing and take a moment to think the situation all the way through. I allowed myself to envision the worst possible outcome and then the best possible outcome. Knowing that my reality would fall somewhere in the middle gave me peace. In this situation, if I wasn't able to hold down a full-time job and pay the bills on my own, the worst possible outcome would be living in a cardboard box on the streets. The best possible outcome would be to admit defeat and go home to Mom. Living with Mom meant no more worrying about putting food on the table, having a built-in babysitter and I could even go back to school. Not too shabby. The middle way would be some version of me working hard and surviving on my own. This little exercise gave me the motivation I needed to take more ownership over the outcome of a given situation. I could sit back and let things happen or I could stand up and forge my own path. Either way, the sun would rise tomorrow whether I was ready for it or not, and so would my son. There was no time for tears or broken hearts. There was work to be done!

When my son was about three, I was working at a bank and was in line for a substantial pay increase. My manager had prepped me before my annual review by saying that I would be very happy with the results. Boy, was she wrong. They totally screwed me over. Not only was I not happy, I left that Friday afternoon meeting feeling disappointed, cheated and unappreciated. I had been doing the work of two people and my numbers showed it. The raises were calculated using a scoring system. Various aspects of our performance were rated on a scale of one to five, with one being the best. In order to even get a cost of living increase, you had to achieve at least 80% of your sales goal. My numbers came in at an astonishing 176% of my sales goal. I was doing the work of two people. My manager could offer no real explanation as to how I scored a two. When asked what I could do differently to get a rating of one the following year, she said, "Just keep doing what you're doing." What a corporate answer! If I had to venture a guess, I would say between the time she told me I would be very happy and the actual review, orders came from higher up the chain to freeze the budget.

Just keep doing what you are doing—those words played over and over in my mind all weekend until something inside me snapped. How much harder would I have to work and not be rewarded? I wanted more than this job could give me. Thankfully, I had enough guts to tell "The Man" to take this job and shove it. On Monday morning, I arrived bright and early with my notice in hand. It was time to jump off the corporate ladder.

You might think that raising a baby at twenty years old would be the scariest thing I'd ever done. However, this was much scarier. I was walking away from my safety net, my dependable, soul sucking full-time job with benefits. This was the first big step I would take out of my comfort zone of mediocrity.

A customer from the bank found out I was leaving and asked me to interview for a receptionist position. It sounded kind of boring. But since I had nothing else lined up, I agreed to meet with her and her business partner. That was the first time I met Bob. He is exactly how you would picture an accountant to look. He even walked and talked the part. Being a receptionist at a tax firm sounded awful, especially if I'd be working with "Mr. Magoo the tax guy," all day. But with bills to pay and a young baby to care for, it made sense to give it a try. Looking for a new job was always an option if this one turned out to be as torturous as I feared.

Well, it wasn't torture, not at all. It was quite the opposite. My inner nerd fell in love with taxes. As luck would have it, I'd completely misjudged the tax guy, too. Bob is one of the coolest people I've ever known. You've never met a more genuine, caring individual as my friend Bob. He's compassionate, appreciative, super smart and hysterically witty. He is also an amazing teacher. We clicked right away and complemented each other's styles rather well.

After only three days of training me, his business partner stopped coming to the office to work. She would come in once a month to pay the bills, including her salary. That was about it. Bob and I were carrying the entire workload. Somehow, we also ended up smack dab in the middle of his partner's messy divorce. It was sad to watch, but even more frustrating to try to work around. We needed to break away. If we wanted to continue to work and serve our clients, we needed to start our own firm.

Our partnership was a match made in heaven. Bob has been coined "a walking tax encyclopedia." There is no one better at negotiating deals with the IRS or navigating through an audit. He certainly has the talent. What he lacks is the ability to navigate the management part of the business. He needed a bossy chick to run the show. As it turns out that's one of my specialties. As a child, all I needed was a group of kids and a ball. Within minutes I'd have them split into teams and playing. I make things happen. That's my super power.

The first thing we needed to do was find an office space to rent. On my first day looking, I found a perfect space for the right price. The next step was furnishing the office. With Mom's help, I found a law firm that was liquidating a giant office full of furniture. I picked up six desks and chairs, three credenzas, nine waiting room chairs, all the mats that go under the desk chairs and a pile of extension cords for only a thousand dollars. (If you've ever bought office furniture, you'd agree this was an amazing deal.) The pieces continued to come together, as if orchestrated by a higher power. Before we knew it, our business was up and running.

Accountants often measure their firm's success by how many personal tax returns they file each tax season. In our first year together, Bob and I prepared 136 returns. That was back in the infancy of our business. Since then we've grown our team to a staff of 10. Over the most recent filing season, our team cranked out over 1,400.

Success is not something you achieve on your own. Just as it takes a village to raise a child, it takes a team to grow a business. We've taken our talents, mixed them with those of an amazing group of people and grown this little tax firm into a high six-figure business.

Our team is a dynamic group of people. Most of them are also super moms. Each of them brings their own strengths and super powers to the table. Whether you're dealing with our Director of First Impressions or our Senior Staff Accountant, you're treated like family. We treat each other like family. This is so different from my days at the bank. Our culture is what I am most proud of. People actually enjoy coming in to get their taxes done. How many accountants can say that?

Time is a precious commodity and I appreciate you spending some of yours to read this. I hope it inspires you to take a step outside of your comfort zone to create or expand your business.

P.S. To this day, when I call Mom to complain about my college age son, she says, "Thought you said it was just a baby?" God, I love that woman.

Melissa Laverty

Melissa was frustrated with corporate bureaucracy when she co-founded Tax Services of Londonderry. She's a problem solver specializing in working with entrepreneurs who struggle with work-life balance. She and her team provide a much-needed reprieve from the plethora of paperwork that chain business owners to their desks. Armed with an uncanny ability to communicate complex information in a clear and concise way, Melissa loves being the office go-to person. She is always engaging the staff to think outside the box. Having lived in Londonderry most of her life, Melissa is well known in the community as a volunteer mom who enjoys hula hooping, camping, and the arts. She is fond of time spent with family, friends and traveling.

Melissa is an Enrolled Agent, QuickBooks Advanced Pro Advisor and member of the following organizations: Northern New England Society of

Enrolled Agents, National Association of Enrolled Agents, Women Inspiring Women and Business Network International.

Melissa Laverty
Tax Services of Londonderry Inc.
1C Commons Dr., Suite 18
Londonderry, NH 03053
603-432-8291
Melissa@tslnh.com
www.TSLNH.com

Jackie Simmons

No Place Left to Hide

You can't be a success and stay a secret.

I know … I tried … for 30 years.

For 30 years, my business felt like a "best-kept secret", almost invisible to the people I most wanted to help. My business was invisible, because *I* was invisible. Like most things in life, being invisible didn't start with being in business.

I became invisible when I was 3. I was invisible the way only a 3-year-old can be.

Have you ever seen a 3-year-old playing hide-n-go-seek? She stands in the middle of the room, scrunches up her little body, and puts her hands over her eyes. She's completely certain that if she can't see you, you can't see her. When you tag her, she jumps and cries in protest, "You can't see me! *I had my eyes closed!"*

When I was 3, I had my eyes closed … by surgery.

While my eyes were bandaged, I "knew" I was invisible. The nurses, not wanting to startle me, spoke softly, took gentle care of me, and I felt safe.

When the bandages came off and I could see again, I knew I wasn't invisible anymore. I returned home to loud angry voices, arguments about money, and military style discipline—the chaos of daily life in my family.

With perfect 3-year-old logic, I decided that being visible wasn't safe.

In my 3-year-old mind, I knew that if I could just get back to being invisible, I would be safe again. I tried covering my eyes, but found I couldn't walk around very well with my hands over my eyes. I tried staying in my room, but it was my sister's room too. If she could see me, others could too.

Finally, I found an answer. I could hide.

Our living room had a green couch on one wall, another green couch on the next wall, and a square table filling the corner between them. I could squeeze my way behind one of the couches, and curl up under the square table. With my red and white blanket around me and my thumb in my mouth, believing that no one could see me, I felt safe.

When I no longer fit under the table, I found other ways to hide.

When I was 5, I tried hiding at a friend's house and not coming straight home from school. It backfired—the levels of fear and anger in the house increased, and my parents fought over whether or not Dad needed to pull off his belt to teach me a lesson.

After that, I learned to hide in plain sight. I "hid" behind books. When I was reading, people left me alone … mostly. I didn't know at the time that I was learning to hide from life … and from myself.

When I was 18, I hid from college behind the busy-ness of getting married and raising kids. When the marriage ended, I continued to hide behind the super-busy-ness of being a single mom and supporting my kids with a home-based business. Building a business, any business, isn't easy. Building a business and staying invisible, is a recipe for struggle and barely getting by.

I had such a strong need to be invisible and feel safe, that not only was my business almost invisible, I was almost invisible—even to myself.

I'd attend networking events, share my knowledge, bring value to the people I'd meet, and then not invite them to work with me (at least not at rates that honored what I did). I could sense what they needed, and willingly shared it with them, thinking that they would magically pay me for the value received, and I wouldn't have to make them (or me) uncomfortable by asking. I'd work for a pittance, grateful for the chance to make money and stay "safe".

Can you relate?

I could walk into a room and tell the emotional state of everyone there. I felt like other people's yucky emotions were sticking to me, as if I was wearing a suit of "Emotional Velcro". It's the opposite of being self-absorbed. Other people's emotions, expectations, and opinions stuck to me and directed me.

There is a dark side to this kind of invisibility. Personally and professionally, it attracts partners who are on the opposite end of the self-absorption scale. You probably know one or two of them. The media calls them narcissists. I prefer to call them: "People who score high on the scale of narcissistic tendencies".

Fancy euphemisms notwithstanding the reality of my second marriage was a dysfunctional, sometimes intimidating home life … again.

I sought help. I spent years with counseling, therapy, and medication— good stuff. I was stable, for a while. I "worked through", "peeled back layers", "let go", and even "forgave"; and still, my marriage was volatile and my business struggled. Don't get me wrong, I am completely grateful for western medicine's body/mind intervention and symptom management. They just couldn't offer me what I wanted. I wanted a cure. So, I went searching in eastern medicine.

Instead of counseling, therapy, and medication, I studied mindfulness, energy, and meditation—good stuff. I deep-dove into that world and came out years later with certifications in multiple energetic healing arts. But, sadly, no cure. In fact, no one even spoke in those terms. I was baffled, confused, and conflicted.

I was baffled because everything I had learned was good stuff, it worked. I was confused because it seemed I needed it all to stay somewhat stable. I was conflicted because now I was in business as a "stress management consultant," using everything I had learned to help others. Yet behind the scenes, my second marriage was falling apart, I was in counseling again, feeling like that scared little girl hiding under the square table in my mom's living room, with my red and white blanket and my thumb in my mouth, afraid of being seen. Still searching for a cure, I studied more.

A mentor explained that each time my ability to stay emotionally present was overwhelmed, the event left behind emotional trash. It was like cooking meals your whole life and never taking the trash out of your kitchen. My "emotional kitchen" was pretty stinky. All of the work I had done on myself was like putting the trash in bags. It didn't take up quite so much room and didn't smell quite so bad ... but it was still there, and it was accumulating.

Every time I started something new, it was like cooking up a gourmet meal and serving it in a pristine dining room, but still being able to smell the trash in the kitchen ... and feeling sure that the other person could smell it too. In fact, I was so sure they could smell my "trash" that I hid from having close relationships. I hid so well that I could pretend I was connected, the same way I pretended to be invisible as a kid.

In my business, the "trash" was like an elephant in the room that sat on my phone so I couldn't make sales calls, trampled my hard work, stunk up my relationships, and kept me distracted and busy so I didn't have to confront how scared I was. Scared that if I shared too much, somehow one of the bags of trash would rip open and I would have to deal with all that emotional mess again. Scared that then everyone else would be able to see my trash and know I was not the sane, confident business woman I projected.

This made no sense to me, I knew my stuff. I created and delivered workshops that helped potential clients be more successful in their own businesses—and then hid from success myself by not doing any follow-ups. I was visible just enough to get by—all the while hiding the fact that I was subsidizing my business with a job, and I was subsidizing my life with anti-depressants.

Then everything changed. My second marriage ended. My youngest child had just graduated high school, and I was halfway through college. In the ensuing chaos, I realized that I had been living someone else's life. I walked away from the degree in business management I'd been pursuing to meet my (now estranged) husband's need for stability. I quit my last W-2 job and I took my last anti-depressant. I thought I was done hiding.

I wasn't. Hiding simply took on new forms. I went into business with a friend, and hid my business brain behind his. I studied two new and powerful arenas, and brought these new skills to enough private clients to know that they were getting amazing results ... but instead of bringing all that expertise to people who would gladly pay me to help them, I hid behind trying to help my trainer and mentor bring *his* work into the world. Between running my friend's business during the week and encouraging my reluctant mentor on the weekends, I had recreated a seemingly predictable life of invisibility.

However, it didn't fit so well this time. I was frustrated with my hiding places. Just like when I could no longer fit under the living room table, I had outgrown my business partner and my mentor.

Through all my study and work on myself, I had finally achieved what I'd been searching for my whole life—freedom from the mental and emotional trash I had been collecting since childhood. I'd succeeded in finding the cure! I had taken out my "trash". The elephant in the room that had been trashing my life was tamed. I was no longer invisible ... and I knew what I wanted!

I wanted to help other women who struggle with invisibility. I wanted to help them permanently remove their emotional trash, and tame the elephants that were keeping their brilliance and their businesses a secret.

All that remained in my way was a lifetime of "hiding" habits.

As they say, "When the student is ready, the teacher will appear." I met a sassy, bossy, in-your-face, completely unashamedly "herself" business woman standing on her own stage making multiple seven figures ... and I knew I had found my coach! I joined a one-year program to work with her towards creating a business making $10,000 a month. That was more than

I had made the whole year before. Determined to succeed, I took action. I brought on replacements to run my friend's business, I stopped pushing my mentor, accepted his blessing, and "launched" … sort of.

I got busy. I was busy in the way only an entrepreneur can be busy.

Have you ever seen an entrepreneur be busy? She sits at her computer for hours researching and writing copy for a website she doesn't know how to build. She hires "help," often friends and family learning to do things – like build websites. She buys tools to automate her marketing and then never gets around to actually reaching out to prospects.

Anything sound familiar? I did all of that. I hid behind the busy-ness of entrepreneurialism, the same way I had hidden behind the busy-ness of single parenthood. My year of business coaching was reaching its end. With three months left to hit my goal, I made a big hairy audacious decision … to sponsor my coach's live event three months away.

30 days later, I knew I was in trouble. I hired more help, professional help this time. In less than two months, we created a clear, concise, compelling message, look, and offer. That launched me on a rocket ride from being a Secret, making almost no money, to a Success.

I closed $6,000 worth of business at the event and then, in the follow-up, had my first ever $10,000 month! Six months later I was on a success panel with New York Times and Wall Street Journal best-selling authors.

Habits can be hard to break.

I went back into hiding behind the entrepreneurial busy-ness … until I was invited to be on a huge livestream, and I woke up to the truth.

I couldn't hide anymore. If I was unwilling to stand up and speak out, I was lying when I said that I wanted to help people.

Facing that hard truth set me off on another rocket ride. I stood up and spoke out and worked with more clients, who started riding their own rockets. I kept notes on what worked. In record time, I turned my notes into a book, and the book into a course. Between them I captured the lessons that moved me from Secret to Success in 7 months and are now helping my clients do the same. (You can read about them, and follow the same steps to your own rocket ride to success, in my book, *Your Path From Secret to Success*.)

For one of my clients, identifying and taming her elephant in the room freed her to move into some quick and powerful action. In our second month, she brought on more clients than she had in the entire history of her business, and ended up making more money in one month than she had made the entire year before.

Another client, after months of feeling overwhelmed, exhausted, and stuck, struggling with one challenging client after another, had a wake-up call and tamed her "elephant". Now she's pulling in clients almost as fast as she can call them—from a list she thought was dead.

There is a comfort and a challenge in knowing that resilience is not a one-time event. Resilience is the willingness to not quit, to challenge your habits, and to stay determined to make a difference. First for yourself and then for the world.

Now it's your turn. How will you come out of hiding, so you can ride your own rocket to success? How will you grow and stay resilient? How will you bounce back no matter how many times your habits, or elephants, try to keep your business hidden?

If you'd like some help charting your success journey, you'll find a worksheet to map out your From Secret to Success path, and some other useful resources, at www.FromSecretToSuccess.com/resilience.

Your rocket ride might be closer than you think.

Jackie Simmons

Being a Secret Can Suck Your Life & Your Business Down the Drain

Removing the "Cloak of Invisibility" from her business skyrocketed Jackie Simmons from Secret to Success in 7 Months. BUT it didn't start out that way.

There's nothing like being an entrepreneur / business owner to stir up an emotional mess!

For Jackie, being a single parent at the same time brought her smack up against mental and emotional blocks that shut her down every time she made progress. These inner saboteurs sat on her phone so she couldn't make sales calls, and distracted her so she couldn't focus and finish projects. They trashed her hard work and torpedoed her relationships.

It was through learning to permanently resolve her own inner blocks that the Total Success Mindset system was born. Jackie used the system to help herself, and then her clients, go From Secret to Success in record time.

Since the 1980's, Jackie has been helping small business owners and entrepreneurs tame the inner saboteurs that trample their profits and productivity and suck their sanity down the drain. In her book *Your Path From Secret to Success*, Jackie guides you through 7 simple steps to a Total Success Mindset—the quickest, most reliable path to becoming the Calm, Focused, Profit-Making Success that you were always meant to be.

Jackie Simmons
From Secret To Success
1748 Chimney Ct.
Sarasota, FL 34235
941-777-4884
Jackie@FromSecretToSuccess.com
FromSecretToSuccess.com/resilience

Nancy Abramovitz

Side Dishes

Stir the Paint

"We need to move," and "We see some suspicious cells." Two sentences that altered my life forever.

How do you heal the broken parts of your life? How do you decide what to focus on and what to get rid of? How do you paint a better picture of your present and future? In the Bible, Timothy is told to fan the flame of his gifts of preaching and teaching. We all have gifts, but sometimes we lose sight of them. An artist at heart, I needed to consider my gifts, and stir the paint.

A Sand Shift

Our many years working in the home furnishings industry were so much fun. I tapped into my creative gifts working as an interior designer for various design firms, in addition to running my own design business. My husband, Jay, was a sales rep for a collection of fine furniture companies, and we assisted each other by lending support and sharing our skills where needed.

We met interesting people from around the world, and furnished our home with beautiful things. These were our best years financially. We enjoyed our lifestyle by dining out, attending theater, including box seats at the Lyric Opera of Chicago, and traveling. We bought gifts for people without worrying about the price tag. We didn't live extravagantly, but we did live well.

We lived in a neighborhood of Chicago that we loved with proximity to downtown, where we spent much of our time. Our home was comfortable, with an attached garage and a large backyard patio for entertaining. We bought it from friends of my grandparents, who were glad we were going to live in the home that her father built. They knew we would take care of it. They toured us around every corner of the yard so we would know the names of everything they'd lovingly planted.

We stretched to buy that house, but things were going so well for us, we knew everything would be okay. This was where we would live for a long time. We decorated, put in central air, and fenced off the yard for our two Old English Sheepdogs. We made plans to remodel the 1950s style kitchen.

Somehow, those remodeling plans never came to fruition. The economy shifted. Our customer bases shifted. Some companies that Jay represented went out of business. High-end furniture became more difficult to sell. Our customers purchased less, and we earned less. The sand was shifting under our feet.

We convinced ourselves that things would turn around, and there was no need to change focus. Jay continued working the lines he had, and I began supplementing my design business by selling window coverings through a company that contracted with large retailers. My idea was to start by selling blinds to folks who might hire me to do interior design work. Instead, the window treatment business took on a life of its own, and I found I had little time for the custom design work that I enjoyed.

As my husband's time became more available due to his dwindling business, he began helping me with mine. What we didn't see was that we spent more time working and were making less money. Pulling money out of savings and retirement accounts, we continued to work our plan, thinking we would be back on top again. We closed our eyes to the fact that we were losing our grasp on what we had built.

We began dining out less, and we cancelled our season tickets to the opera. We stayed home more, turned down invitations to go out and stayed with the current work plan. But it wasn't enough. At some point, it became apparent that we could no longer keep up with the mortgage payments. We were living beyond our means and had to put on the brakes.

We were no longer living in abundance. We were living in scarcity. We became people who found ourselves asking what things cost and feeling nervous about spending money. We needed to move. We held garage sales and donated loads of things to charities as we packed up and left our home.

Finding "Framily"

When my husband announced he was going to attend a job fair, I couldn't believe my ears. We had been in denial about him having to make a career change, and we were "allergic" to traditional employment. What would he find that suited him at a job fair? Interestingly, at the very moment we were ready to give up our independence and get "regular jobs," a new opportunity revealed itself.

One of the booths at the job fair was staffed by members of a real estate investing community. Having an interest in real estate investing, we were open to the idea. The cool thing was, they offered investing education, and they were local. Because we were fearful about investing on our own, we had never invested in real estate before, other than buying our own house. This group was different. They offered professional training, coaching and mentorship. We could now truly be in business for ourselves, but not by ourselves. On top of that, there was a referral program that allowed us to tap into our expertise in marketing, and that enabled us to develop multiple income streams.

We jumped in and haven't looked back. What we found is a nationwide community of real estate investors with a large local presence. We found a "framily"—friends who are like family. There is no competitive angst, and no boss or sales manager to answer to. Instead, there is support, camaraderie and love. We truly care about each other, we learn together and we work together. We've learned about real estate investing and how to run our business. We've learned to overcome the scarcity mindset. We've learned to develop income systems. We continue to learn every day, and I can utilize my gifts of helping and training. This time, we made the shift ourselves, instead of the shift happening to us.

While we were sad to leave our home in the city, we had an opportunity to move into a newly renovated 1902 Victorian house in the far suburbs. Did it have an attached garage and big patio like we used to have? No. There also was not enough room for all of the beautiful furniture we had collected over the years. We traded space for a different kind of charm. Although we felt lucky to find this situation through great friends in our investing community, my gratefulness was being overshadowed by what we had to give up.

We both missed the city, the theater and being close to friends and family. I missed the Merchandise Mart, the restaurants, and the lake. I needed to work on shaking the self-pity and instead see the miracles all around me. We had to own up to our part in what was happening to us and focus on what we could change.

In the rehabbing business, we say if one door closes, we can knock through a wall and create a brand-new door. Our business was going well but our attitudes still needed work. As any business venture goes, we dipped, then excelled, dipped, then excelled. It's been interesting finding our stride.

Along the way, we were introduced to a lot of personal-development training. Becoming better people is essential to becoming better business people. We've enjoyed leadership opportunities and recognition for many achievements along the way. We have learned how to think about money differently. We think about building wealth instead of just earning a paycheck. We have found a home with this community and are now grateful every day that we discovered this opportunity to rebuild.

Our business is still not where we want it to be, but it's getting there. I spent a good deal of time toward the end of 2016 considering what we need to do to have our business gain momentum faster. I knew we were not destined to live a life of mediocrity. I also knew we had to turn our past disappointments into opportunities. We needed to use our abilities to communicate, inspire and help other people in order to help ourselves.

The Big Jolt

As life happens, 2016 ended with a mixture of celebration and sadness. Just prior to Christmas, we received news that one of our dearest friends died while on his way to Chicago to spend time with his family and Christmas Day with us. Although we felt profound sadness at his passing, our holiday plans were already in motion. We proceeded to celebrate Christmas with family and friends. We cried and laughed as we celebrated our friend's life and the impact he had on all of us.

I had a specific agenda for the week between Christmas and New Year's. I planned to relax and reflect on the blessings as well as the sadness of 2016. I planned to regroup about how the New Year would start off with a bang in our business. We were excited to jump in and do big things in 2017. This was to be the year we would take our business to the next level. I had also scheduled appointments for medical checkups between the holidays before our insurance plan changed on January 1st.

I felt good, and was certain that all would check out well. Quite unexpectedly, however, we ended 2016 with a major jolt. The call came an hour after my mammogram to tell me they saw some suspicious cells and I needed to consult a surgeon. I was not prepared.

We spent January in a whirlwind of tests and doctor consultations. At first, we told very few people what was going on. I was on unfamiliar ground with my emotions. Several years before, I had hip replacements, and that was a piece of cake. I knew that I would get new joints, the pain would go away and I would be able to get around much better. It was all positive. But this was something different.

My diagnosis was pre-invasive breast cancer. The very words were hard to say. My doctor said it had to be taken care of, but in its current state, it would not kill me. Good news. If left alone, it could become invasive and become much harder to treat. Bad news. I quipped to her that this may not kill me, but my husband might kill me for putting him through it!

I felt sad and out of control. In consultations with my doctors, I would get the facts, make decisions and then begin to melt. My throat closed, my eyes welled with tears and I couldn't breathe. Thankfully, I had my husband by my side, who was my rock and my best friend. Before surgery, I didn't tell many people because I didn't want them feeling sorry for me. I needed to steel myself for the impending procedure. I decided to treat this as a project. Lay out the terms, consider what had to be done and in what order. That was how I could get through it.

I survived the mastectomy and reconstruction. Being in the rehab business, this was not exactly the kind of reconstruction I had bargained for!

I laid low for several weeks to recuperate. People sent food, flowers, prayer blankets, books and fun things to occupy my time. Texts, calls, cards, prayers and emails from family and friends were a blessing.

It was no coincidence that months earlier I made a friend on Facebook from church who had gone through a similar experience. We kept in constant contact during my ordeal, which was a tremendous help. She gave me advice, encouragement and prayers. My husband, sisters, the moms and other family members kept me bolstered. My small tribe of people were there for me. One call that I received surprised me. The CEO of our investment education company called to wish me well, offer his prayers and any help I might need. How cool was that? Most people would fear being fired if they had to take a month off. Instead, I received prayers.

During recovery, I read books, watched movies, napped, and did a lot of thinking. There's a grieving that goes with losing a body part, but a gratefulness that dangerous cells were detected, extracted, and I would go on to live a long and healthy life. I decided to focus on the future, not my current condition.

Life Is Like a Turkey Dinner

The word that kept going through my mind during those weeks was healing. I had a lot of healing to do. I realized I had more than just physical healing to do, which prompted me to make a list, as is my modus operandi. I looked at all the parts of my life that needed healing. I realized that for me to be whole, I needed to heal my thoughts and spirit. I read, I prayed and I thought. I thought about another one of my gifts, hospitality.

I pride myself on putting together a great Thanksgiving dinner. I plan, organize and make lists for weeks. Our guests contribute favorite dishes. It's a meal with many components. It must be balanced for everything to come out at the right time, and temperature.

Many people feel anxious preparing this holiday meal. The major task is getting just the right turkey. You prepare it, dress it, roast it, watch it, baste it, watch it some more, carve it, plate it and garnish it. Then you serve it!

But what about the side dishes? If you focused only on the turkey, would the mashed potatoes get soupy and the green bean casserole burn? Would the gravy get lumpy and would you forget about the rolls in the freezer?

You're exhausted from pulling it all together. People gather at the table but you forget to write a beautiful prayer of Thanksgiving. Maybe you fumble for the right words, but your message isn't as meaningful as you'd hoped.

You serve the food, and by the time you sit down, the guests are ready for second helpings. You are up and down, barely taking a bite. As you begin to relax and enjoy the conversation of loved ones, the kids get cranky and people ask to be excused from the table. Is dessert ready?

When the guests go home, you mull over the day, thinking about how things could have gone better. If you had prepared more in advance, or asked for more help, would you have been calmer and not so exhausted? If you had planned better and concentrated on the spirit of the holiday and giving thanks, might this have been a more successful holiday?

Over the years, I have developed many holiday hacks to make things go smoother. It's the same with life. If you can better balance your side dishes, e.g., your physical, spiritual, emotional and financial components, might your life feel calmer?

I thought about our business and saw that if I only focused on making our business grow (the turkey), but didn't work on my emotions, thoughts, and spirit, (the side dishes), I would fail at my attempts. I realized that I needed to let go of the sadness about what we left behind when we moved. I had to get rid of the sadness over my surgery. I had to make time for things that gave me joy, like my artwork, reading and getting out more. We could find local entertainment that didn't have to cost as much. I didn't have to feel deprived. I would make time for things that rounded out my life, and in doing so, my spirit and thoughts would be much healthier. My mind would be in a better place to make my business healthier.

Like the lists I make when I prepare my Thanksgiving dinner, I now make lists for my life. What side dishes do I need to make my life more fulfilling? By accepting personal responsibility in life, and showing your scars, you can heal yourself and your business.

Look at your own life and make a list of all the parts that are important to you. How balanced is your attention to each part? Break it down. Make sub-lists. As you think about your own business, I invite you to pay attention, not just to the perfect turkey, but to all the side dishes in your life that make you whole. What needs healing for you?

The Living List

Below is my personal Healing List. After each item I detail what I need to work on to achieve healing in that area. This is a living list that changes as I make shifts in my life.

Physical: A healthy diet, exercise and attention to physical well-being.

Spiritual: Strengthen my faith, make time for my art and creative hobbies.

Emotional: Practice positive thinking and keep gratefulness in my thoughts.

Relationship:	Spend quality time with friends and family.
Education:	Keep learning; read, listen and pay attention.
Financial:	Plan to earn what I need and want, and decide what I don't need.
Business:	Be open to opportunities and possibilities, budget time, money and make big plans.

Today, many of us work in network marketing businesses. We're in the business of helping people solve their problems and ease their pain. As we build our teams, it's certain that people are less interested in working with someone who is carrying around old, painful baggage. They are more interested in working with people who are positive, passionate, and painting the picture of a bright future. Be that person and you will heal your business instantly.

Because of my healing list, I'm focusing on the side dishes, stirring the paint, and creating a new picture for my life. Come join me!

One of my favorite quotes is by Daniel Burnham, "Make no little plans; they have no magic to stir men's blood."

Nancy Abramovitz

Nancy Abramovitz resides in the Chicagoland area with her husband, Jay. They run BTE Ventures, Inc., a company dedicated to building and inspiring a nationwide community of independent real estate investors and marketers. Their purpose is to create opportunities for financial stability and financial freedom for themselves and others.

Nancy and her husband serve on the Executive Leadership Committee for their local real estate investing community, and are 5-Star Qualified Affiliates for the #1 real estate investment education program in the country.

Nancy is a member of the Northwest Suburban Toastmasters Club, where she continues to sharpen her public speaking skills. She is also a proud supporter of the Responsibility Foundation and the Statue of Responsibility movement. She is helping to raise awareness of this important project and hopes that everyone will understand its importance and become part of the movement. www.responsibilityfoundation.org/

Nancy is an on-going student of the art of real estate investing, a graduate of Eastern Illinois University and The International Academy of Interior Design. She is also a licensed interior designer.

She has completed the Conscience Producer self-development course, and continues to study a variety of self-development programs. In addition, Nancy is an artist, dog-lover, and proponent of animal welfare. She loves to read, cook, and is a music and theater enthusiast.

For more information about how you can change the trajectory of your financial path through real estate investing, legal entity structuring, tax mitigation and interest reduction, all with the help and support of a community of awesome people, please contact Nancy here: nancy.bte.biz@gmail.com.

Nancy and Jay are both public speakers and would welcome the opportunity to speak to your group about healing, real estate investing, financial liberation and overcoming your life of mediocrity.

Nancy Abramovitz
BTE Ventures
nancy.bte.biz@gmail.com
312-286-1583
www.BTEVentures.Biz
www.incomesystemsforlife.com

Ylona Cavalier

RISE & SHINE—
The Good Lord Is Upon Us!

I was a four-year-old little girl who was taken abroad with her only sister, Simona, mom and dad. "I LOVE AMERICA!" my dad would say. Just after getting out of the Army, while the communists were trying to take over Czechoslovakia, we escaped and fled to Austria. My dad left his whole family behind, including his mother, father, relatives and friends. We hid in a boot camp in Austria for six months, flew to New York City, stayed there for only a short couple of days and then flew to Cleveland, Ohio, where we stayed for three years. My brother, Claude Stetka, was born in Cleveland. We then moved to Chicago and have lived here ever since. I suppose I've gotten some of my courage from my father, who was very adventurous and direct.

I have been in the fitness industry since I was sixteen years old. A stranger at a gym called Women's Workout World in Berwyn, IL inspired me. She said, "You're really great at how you exercise. You should become a fitness trainer."

Twenty-eight years later, here I am. I love teaching fitness classes and doing personal training. It is my passion. It releases endorphins, which make me feel alert, alive and great. Who doesn't like to look good in the mirror? "It feels great to be fit. I love to look great, don't you?" I have always been pretty thin, but the belly thang has always been a poochy problem. My whole life I've lost and gained the same ten to twenty pounds over and over again. Over the past forty years, I have always seemed to be on some kind of new fad diet. I was feeling stressed after always being asked if I was pregnant because of my poochy belly. I, therefore, decided to do something about it. After attending a Mind, Body, Spirit show in Chicago, I met a friend who introduced me to PURIUM. They produce all organic superfoods, nutrition and supplements to make a body good. It is great, healthy, ALL ORGANIC superfood nutrition and is excellent fuel for our bodies. After doing a ten-day transformation, which consists of detoxifying, cleansing, nourishing and re-energizing my body, I was ready to get back into my bikini. Just like spring cleaning your house yearly, it is good to detox and cleanse our bodies too. This is truly not a diet. It is a lifestyle transformation change. I have been searching many years for an all organic superfood company and found many chemicals in many brands except PURIUM. We must pay attention to "OTHER" ingredients on the labels—they are not good, and if we cannot pronounce the words, we probably should not be ingesting them. I am ever so grateful and thankful to have finally found an all organic superfood that makes me feel great, look fantastic and gives me energy. My website is: www.ylonacavalier.com. Go browse my website, and if you see something you like, here's a $50 gift card for you. Your gift card code is: leopard. That's $50 off anything of your choice. It is my gift to you!

In addition to wonderful superfood nutrition, I feel that keeping the body at a healthy, high vibrational state is imperative and important. I am excited to have been introduced to fabulous aromatherapy. Young Living Essential Oils is the BEST company and one hundred percent therapeutic. I have seen miraculous results from these fabulous oils with myself, my family and my friends. Do yourself and your family a favor and get the toxicity out of your life. Please remember that Jesus was anointed by Frankincense and Myrrh at the inn when he was born. You can view amazing oils at: www.youngliving.com. My Young Living member number is 3086522. Call me at 630-201-1755 for more information or to attend a Healthy Happy Hour monthly meeting.

There have been some challenges in life that I've been through. Between 2001 and 2012, there were many deaths in our family. Almost all of them were under the young age of sixty. I lost my best friend, Kim, to a blood clot in the heart at thirty-eight years old, watched my forty-three-year-old sister,

Simona, die of a brain aneurysm, lost my wonderful grandmother at seventy-five years of age to a brain aneurysm and saw my forty-five-year-old sister-in-law, Barbara, die of shock to the heart. My sixty-year-old step-mom, Anne, died of liver, lung and brain cancer, my dad, Stanley, died from a rare disease called amyloidosis and my sixty-five-year-old Aunt Liba died of cancer. My father-in-law, Bob, died of brain cancer, and my mom is now suffering from the effects of a stroke at the young age of fifty-nine. My mother, Ylona Stetka, cannot walk or talk and is paralyzed on the right side of her body. She is now seventy-two years old. All of this makes me want to help others. I am overcome by compassion and want to help others to strive for better health. I love to lift people up, make them laugh and feel great about themselves.

I have also been through some difficult challenges with my three sons. I watched all three boys come into this world with severe issues. My oldest son, Zachary, was born with a hole in his heart and a hydro-seal. My second son, Joshua, was born with pneumonia and was in the hospital for ten days after his birth. My youngest son, Max, was born two months premature. He was diagnosed with mal-rotation, bowel obstruction and twisted intestines. He had four surgeries and spent sixty days at Children's Memorial Hospital in Chicago. Max almost died. Dr. Luck, a gastrointestinal surgeon, saved his life. This really made me think about health. We must take care of our bodies, since they are our temple. If you don't have your health, you don't have a great life ahead of you.

There were even more challenges. In 2003, I was in a fatal car accident. A semi-truck hit my car on the highway, which forced me into the cement median. The right side of my face was crushed (it is now being held together by 17 screws four steel plates), my L4 vertebrae was crushed and my left wrist was broken. I had to wear a body brace from my neck to my waist for my back to heal. After a five-hour reconstructive surgery to repair my face, I am indebted to Dr. Kopolovic who put me back together again. I knew at this point, I had a new chance at life. It was a renewal of my birth. It was a second chance to make my life better and to help the lives of others around me. I am

BLESSED and ever so THANKFUL to be alive! I AM full of FAITH, hope and joy from the Lord above. He is my ROCK, my savior and my stronghold. Without faith and the love of GOD and the Holy Spirit, I could not go on. I am also blessed with the wonderful friendships I've made over the first half of my life.

Corporate America is challenging. It has been a long haul in corporate America. I AM finally done with that phase of my life. After being pushed around for so many years, it has drained my energy. GOD said there is something better for me. Something else He wants me to do with the second half of my life, which is going to be better than the first half. I have been fired for peeing. I lost my job because they told me I wasn't good enough after landing an $800,000 deal and achieving the biggest box lunch order ever for a catering company. I once again lost my job at an Engineering Firm to the president's son. This was the last straw for me. I prayed earnestly about what to do with my life. I have decided to go into business for myself. My heart feels great when I am able to help others who are less fortunate than I am.

My passion is to uplift, de-stress and help others get on their way to a happier, healthier, fitter, better, sun-shiny goodness! I am fully aware that GOD wants me to be happy. He wants me to travel, be financially free and be able to go to all of these great beaches all across this GOD given earth.

Our time is NOW! This is the time and the theme of satisfaction, comfort and grounding. I am anxiously excited to bless others with avalanches of spiritual blessings along with helping others with great, healthy options. I love to inspire all of my family, relatives I have left and my ever so wonderful, super-fantastic friends. NOW is the time to travel, read a book, relax and take more vacations in my life with my family, including my husband, John, and my three wonderful sons.

I wish to dedicate this chapter and book to my wonderful mom, Ylona Stetka, my husband, John Cavalier, my three super great sons, Zachary, Joshua and Max Cavalier, and my one and only best brother, Claude Stetka. I would also like to thank my wonderful, super-fantastic friends along with my super-great fitness trainer, Mr. Maurice McBryde at Bring It! Fitness in Westmont, IL. With his wisdom, knowledge and patience, he has helped me achieve many fitness goals and dreams in 2017 and I hope he will continue to do so in the future. Avalanches of blessings to you all!

2017 and beyond will be a time of great financial success, financial freedom and new beginnings of new, fantastic relationships. This year and in all future years, we will be confident, strong, faithful and full of excitement and vigor.

I look forward to helping myself and YOU succeed! I am excited to be financially free. With my continued faith, I KNOW good things are coming my way and are truly possible. I eagerly want to share this faith with everyone I meet. I am excited and thankful for the richness in my heart. I am ever so grateful for the wonderful adventures, relationships and AVALANCHES OF BLESSINGS GOD has in store for me and you today, tomorrow and every day.

DECLARE BLESSINGS FOR YOURSELF

"Say to them, may the Lord bless you and protect you, may the Lord smile upon you and be gracious to you, may the Lord show you His favor and give you His peace."—Numbers 6:23–26

A blessing is not a blessing until it is declared, so today, declare a blessing over yourself and others. Speak that blessing in the name of Jesus. Declare you are blessed with GOD's supernatural wisdom and receive clear direction for your life. Declare today that you are blessed with creativity, courage, talent and abundance. You are blessed with a strong will, self-control and self-discipline. You are blessed with a great family, great friends, great health, faith, favor and fulfillment. You are blessed with success, supernatural strength, promotion and divine protection. You are blessed with a compassionate heart and a positive outlook on life. Declare that any curse or negative word that's ever been spoken over you is broken right now in the name of Jesus. Declare that everything you put your hand on is going to prosper and succeed. Declare today and every day. (Deuteronomy 28:1–14)

Here is a **PRAYER FOR YOU TODAY**: Precious Father, thank you for speaking blessings over my life in your word. Thank you for equipping me with everything that I need to be successful. Teach me to consistently believe in and declare your blessings over my life and the lives of those around me.

AMEN

GOD BLESS YOU!

Ylona Cavalier

Photo by My Great Friend Radek Thor

Ylona Cavalier is a dynamic fitness group exercise instructor, personal trainer and organic gardener. Ylona has been in the fitness industry since 1983. Ylona holds specialty certifications in Cardio/Aerobics, Hatha Yoga, Spinning, Tabata, Core, Gliding, TRX Suspended weight training and the Doxa Soma-Praise Body-Christian Exercise Practice of integration of prayer, worship and stretching. Ylona received her 200 hour yoga certification at Soderworld Healing Arts & Spa Center located in Willowbrook, Illinois.

In addition to fitness, Ylona also studies nutrition with her new company PURIUM-ALL organic superfoods. It is 80% nutrition what we put into our mouths and 20% exercise. Please take a look and browse her website at: ylonacavalier.babystepseo.com

Ylona has taught fitness classes at Good Samaritan Health and Wellness

Center for 10 years, Edwards Health and Fitness Center in Woodridge and Naperville for eight years and the new ARC-Athletic Recreation Center in Woodridge, IL. Ylona's teaching style is truly an uplifting, enthusiastic and fun workout experience.

Ylona Cavalier
PURIUM & YOUNG LIVING Essential Therapeutic Oils
630-201-1755
ycavalier@comcast.net
www.ylonacavalier.com
ylonacavalier.babystepseo.com

Dorci Hill

It Takes Guts to Find Your Glory

I didn't have a horrible childhood. Nor did I have a horrific illness that affected me for the rest of my life. You could say my life was idyllic, because it was! Yet, in every life there is a story and it doesn't always stem from or linger in the ugly, dark side of life. My story was born from love and thrives today. The form and players have changed, yet the sentiment remains steadfast. You see, I was adopted—and yes—I know just how COOL that is!!! To be wished for so desperately that nothing on earth will fill that void, is a heavy burden albeit a wonderful one. I still have the letter that my parents received from the adoption agency telling them that they had been APPROVED FOR ADOPTION! Oh My GOSH! Doesn't that give you goosebumps??? It does to me even now. I tell people that although I didn't come from her body, I came from my mother's heart and that is where she remains with me today. Sadly, my story does have a bit of a hiccup. She became ill and passed away at 47 years of age, just before my 22nd birthday. My heart, my life and my love was taken from me before I could do anything of value. I was still in college and had not started my life yet. How was she to ever see what I would do, say, become or believe? And how would she ever hear my cries to her mixed with sadness and joy about all that I was experiencing? They say that absence makes the heart grow fonder and they (whomever the heck THEY are!) are right! I love her more today than I ever thought possible. The mother that resides in me, reflects the woman that she was in life. All I am today is possible because of the love and sacrifice that she endured. She shaped my view of the world. She also gave me the strength to know that anything is possible because she was there for me, regardless of the form she now takes. I firmly believe in life beyond death and when I need her, she is still there. She visits from time to time in my dreams, in smells that only a memory can touch, in the Elvis songs and movies we loved to watch (YES—I was and still am an Elvis fan! I mean come on—he's a hunka hunka burnin' love for crying out loud!).

I give all the credit to her for the path I now follow. As a dancer from the ripe old age of 4, I had always figured that I would make my way to a performing/visual arts high school and then on to stardom on stage and screen. That would take a backseat, when her illness struck. I was in college on a dance scholarship, flirting with the notion of becoming a chiropractor or possibly a medical doctor. "IT" happened during my junior year of college and after several months of unexplained symptoms with zero relief from numerous medications, they decided to put her into the hospital and perform exploratory surgery to see exactly what was going on. Upon opening her up, they determined that there was nothing they could do. They stitched her back together and gave us an early glimpse of the grim reaper. The big "C" had come to call. You see, she was diagnosed with a rare form of internal melanoma, (skin cancer—Inside her??? My thoughts exactly! It was a "what the heck" are you talking about kind of moment when I heard that diagnosis), and it would take her from me in less than 5 months. She wouldn't see me graduate from college, get married or live the life I was destined to live. It was all because her journey ended, while mine continued. She died, I live. Or did I? Do any of us live beyond the death of a cherished one? We eventually do, although to what degree is questionable. I know that typically you are supposed to lose a parent before yourself. It was just way too damn early. Soooo, I faltered, a bit. I married someone I shouldn't have, took a job in a field that was in line with my degree that I didn't love and slowly over the years shuttered my heart, passion and desire until it was locked up tight and forgotten. The best part of me that was her had died.

Luckily, I am a bit of a hard-headed woman! For you sign loving folks—I am an Aries—explanation enough! It didn't take me too long to realize that I was being stifled and caged. I was not honoring the woman in her and the mother that remained in me, by NOT living a life full out. I, therefore, divorced that brain-fart after 3 years, left that dead-end job in a biological testing facility and began my journey into a life of health, wellness and entrepreneurship! This was honoring her and more importantly listening to and tapping into my inner guide. Those gut feelings that always tell you when you are doing the "heart" thing rather than the "head" thing. For it is in following the heart, that our true passion and purpose lies.

I had made a pact prior to coming here, to fulfill certain tasks and I had gotten lost. I was lost in my grief, because love and grief know no time. I went from being sure of myself and knowing no fear, to being fearful of stepping out as the true source of all that I had been gifted and tasked with providing to this world during my time here. (Side note, if anyone tells you to "just get over it already" after the loss of a loved one, tell them simply to "shut the hell up!" and quickly find another friend! Grief is personal and healing time is personal. You cannot put time limits on deep feelings and a lifetime connection.)

My mother's battle brought forth the desire to seek out better – better ways to be healthy, better ways to be treated, better ways to live life full out and better ways to just be. There have been many fits and starts along the journey and many late night heavenly calls to her—of which, in her way, she answered. I know that in all my "schemes", she is there guiding me and cheering me onward. I know how proud she always was of anything I did. I also know that she is still gently guiding me. That unfortunately makes it even more difficult when I stumble and travel back down the path of confusion, second-guessing and doubt. Those are hard core filters to break free from and a mindset that is hard to change. I have done so many things in my life thus far to be proud of—dancing from the age of 4 through college; performing on TV at the Aloha Bowl in Hawaii; modeling for several years; graduating with 2 degrees; briefly having a craft store; starting a cleaning service with 25 employees when I sold it—just to name a few proud moments!

So why then, is it so hard to believe in myself as completely as she always did? It is because I started listening to others who have not done much with their lives, who stopped dreaming and had not stretched their belief that they not only could have more—they deserved more. I had always known that I had been given a great many talents and that there were big things in store for me. I never dream small! Why should I, when the stars in the heavens that I look up to are themselves infinite? Our mind loves to keep us comfortable in a safe place that we know and are familiar with, doesn't it? It is so much easier to remain in my little "comfort zone", instead of stepping out as who I really am and letting everyone see ME, hear ME, know ME. What if they don't like ME, respect ME or follow ME? It is easier to NOT be ME and shrink before I shine. That belief alone is not honoring her nor allowing myself to be the beautiful, accomplished being that I am. The one thing that keeps me going forward, is the faith of my mother that I could do whatever it was my heart led me to and accomplish it with a flair all my own. It is time to "suck it up buttercup" and get this global party started!

It is my belief that we come to everything in life at the exact moment we are supposed to. I now find it ironic that I am FINALLY stepping out fully into my true being the very year I turn 47. It is the exact age that she attained before being called to a higher purpose. Ironic or destiny? I prefer to call it on time and ready to rock my global message! I never gave up, even though many times it would have been easier to continue to live with the thoughts of "Why would anyone ever listen to me? Choose me? Hear me?" It took guts to stay the course, learn the lessons and develop the lifetime of skills to deliver my message the way it is meant to be heard. It comes from the heart, with a lifetime of my mother's love beating strongly behind it. Don't get me wrong, there are still days when I feel frozen in a sea of concrete and I am unable to move beyond my fear of HOW will it turn out and HOW will it happen. I know that the fear of remaining the same, in the same place a year from now, scares me more than the fear of not being able to see the HOW. I simply cannot move backwards or remain still. Neither should you. Life is meant to be lived full out and full on. Even to live simply—to know who you are and be perfectly okay telling the world this is me, takes guts! I finally realized that I am stronger than my fear, I am beautiful because I am here, my life has a purpose and there's no better time than now to let it all out!

It may not always be easy. Anything worth having is worth the pain or fear to get it here. Warts and all, guts and all. It's time to be realistic and go for the life of my dreams. My "gut" is telling me to (as my beloved nanny always told me) "Poop or get off the pot!" I am starting so small that I cannot fail. It requires simple steps forward each day toward my dreams. That's all it takes. One simple step at a time. The fear fades away, the HOW takes care of itself, and then I find myself writing, speaking, coaching and stepping onto the world stage as I always knew I would. And that is where I find you. I am ready...are you?

I penned this on behalf of my mother when she passed in 1992. I hope you enjoy it as much as I enjoyed writing this in her memory.

> *"Memories float like dreams across the window of my heart.*
> *The details escape me but the colors remain.*
> *Day dawns,*
> *envelopes my world,*
> *takes hold of my heart...and flies."*

Never be afraid to fly. If you need someone to hold you, I am there. If you need someone to believe in you, I am there. Just as she was and still is for me, I am ready, now, to be the woman and mother she was to me, for you. Reach out your hand and take a walk with me into your waking dreams. It takes guts to be glorious and together we can shine bright so that others may do the same.

Dorci Hill

A healthy lifestyle is more than a "diet". There is no such thing as a "One plan fits all" approach. As a realistic wellness lifestyle expert, Dorci works together with her clients to develop a lifestyle of healthy choices that is based on their realistic view of where they are now, where they would like to be and more importantly, the steps they are willing to take to achieve this goal. Her specialty is in discovering and prioritizing her clients' First Steps into a lifetime of health and wellness. She believes that lasting health should be attainable, affordable and a priority for living the life her clients deserve. The start is the stop for most people. Her passion is for everyone to achieve their desired vision of a healthy lifestyle. By tapping into her 18+ years of health and wellness, body mechanics and movement experience, she can then create a plan is that is both sustainable and feasible for each person. She feels that after all, "Every body is different. It's your health, your life and your plan." That is what makes the lasting difference!

Dorci earned two degrees—an Associates of Arts and a B.S. in Biology/Chemistry. She was a dancer from the age of 4 through college. She practices yoga and pilates and is working on a certification in Ballet Barre. Dorci is also the 5th licensed facilitator in the United States of the Certified Healing Dance Therapy—Chakradance™.

She holds retreats, group coaching sessions, one on one coaching and basic accountability groups. She also volunteers with several animal rescue groups and has "adopted" a mentally challenged gentleman at a local home for the disabled for the past 15 years.

Dorci Hill
Dorci Hill Global Wellness
1921 Parkcrest St.
Alvin, TX 77511
832-425-9090
dorci@dorcihillglobal.com
www.dorcihillglobal.com

Marci D. Toler

Lead Strong, Serve Selflessly, Be Your Best Self and Love Well—Lessons from Iraq

We had finally boarded the plane, we had made it! All of the work, worry, struggle, arguments, and training were finally over. We were heading overseas. We were heading to Iraq by way of Kuwait in the fall of 2008. I remember that I had removed my boots for the 15-hour flight, and I had my feet on the bulkhead, settling in for the flight. I remember thinking "Good God... what have you done?" Literally, "God—Big Guy, Lord & Savior, Maker of the Universe—what have you done?"

I am not good enough.

I do not know what I am doing.

I have not deployed here before - and you put me in command. . .

What were you thinking?

I mean, I am not a great Soldier, I mean really. . . I cannot shoot well, I am not very "Hooah", I am a mother of three, I am over 40.... and remember, I no longer do the 2-mile run... I do the alternate 2.5 mile walk because of my knees. I am not the poster-child Army officer.

I am demanding. I lose my temper. I get tired. I do not always play well with others. I do not always play inside the box. What have you done?

I had taken command of the 259th Combat Sustainment Support Battalion in December 2007. We mobilized July 11, 2008 for a 12-month rotation to support Operation Iraqi Freedom. I was taking 75 Army Reserve Soldiers from across the United States, to assume command of what would become the largest battalion in Iraq with over 1,700 Soldiers and 635 contractors; across all three components of the service, Active, National Guard and Reserve, and throw in a few Navy Sailors for good measure.

I remember looking at my senior non-commission officer, my battle buddy, and thinking I cannot fail him and I'm sure I will.

All I could think as I was trying desperately not to cry was... "Okay God, you got me here, I'm going to need your help. Just don't let me make a fool of myself, let me come home to my family and help me bring these Soldiers home."

We had landed in Kuwait. I stood off to the side of the aircraft watching Soldiers from my unit and another we had picked up along the way, come down the stairs carrying their packs, pillows, and weapons. I turned away for a split second—and heard someone yell. A Soldier from the other unit had lost his balance with his load and fell head first down the stairs. All I know about him, was that he was moved off to the medical treatment facility, and never made it into the fight. I do not know how seriously hurt he was, or how he is today. It was a split-second, a moment, and his plan changed. I was just thankful it was not one of my Soldiers, and moved out to make sure we were accounted for, and ready to move.

It lingers in my memory as a reminder that we can be prepared, we can be walking into our story, and lose our balance for just a moment and never make it into the fight.

Every unit stops in at a training base in Kuwait to adjust to the time zone, the heat, complete a weapons check and finish some training. As airlift becomes available, units are moved north into their mission area to assume responsibility for the mission. While we were in this transition phase, an aviation brigade was moving into the fight with us. They were completing their shakedown flights after receiving their helicopters off the ships that had transported them from the States. We were completing our required training.

It was an ordinary day, in the middle of extraordinary circumstances. Then, it wasn't. We knew something had gone terribly wrong, when all our training had been cancelled and we were just told to hold tight in our housing area (tents in the desert). They had a helicopter go down, and the flight crew had been killed.

In a flash, in a heartbeat... training turns to disaster... routine turns to failure.... life turns to death.

We hadn't even made it to Iraq yet!

After nearly a month in Kuwait... maybe it wasn't that long... but it felt that way, sleeping with 30 of my closest female friends in a tent designed for 20, in the Kuwaiti heat, cooled by generator powered air conditioner units that only had two settings: full blast, or off.... fighting boredom and trying to keep Soldiers focused and ready... that month was an odd combination of fear of the unknown, fear of failure, and leading from a place of confidence. I often felt like I was not worthy, not good enough and faking my way. Maybe everyone felt that way, but no one showed any known weakness. We made promises to each other. Things like, "No matter what happens, tell my children I was very brave", or "It's 2008, it's very, very safe!", while we waited to go further north into the active combat zone. We finally moved...albeit I think it was over a course of a week, before we finally all made it up north, but we were in Iraq. We were acting, moving forward.

It was my first night in Iraq, and I was headed to my room in an old Iraqi storage building that had been converted to house four rooms. There was no running water, but I had power, my own room and I had a television with the Armed Forces Network and air conditioning. I had a bed, a closet and a chair. And in a few days, I would have my own vehicle... Living large in Joint Base Balad!!

But that night I once again was asking God what he was thinking. . . this was me, what was I doing in Balad, Iraq, preparing to take command of, at the time, eight companies and over 1,000 Soldiers, in this place where Abraham was born? In a place of history, in a place dominated by men on and off the base. Did I mention that I was just an over 40 mom that did this Army thing part-time? I knew in my heart there was no going back. I was committed—but I was scared. I was afraid that I would fail. I would fail my Soldiers. I would fail those who believed in me back home. I would fail my family. I would fail myself.

I wish I could say that I heard a great voice of comfort, or that the sky opened and I saw the light. No.... instead I saw a sandstorm coming, and the night settling in. I took a deep breath and walked into my room.

Sometimes, all you can do is send up a prayer, take a deep breath and keep walking.

We assumed the mission in the traditional Transfer of Authority ceremony from the 13th Combat Sustainment Support Battalion on September 12, 2008, and transferred it to the 80th Ordnance Battalion on June 17, 2009.

During those months, we managed four logistical support and distribution activities. We supplied over $39 million worth of supplies to 326 war fighter units across Northern Iraq, as we fought to maintain the gains made during the 2007 surge of forces. We established the first-ever U.S. Government contract to be given to an Iraqi businessman which, over the course of the contract, saved $100 million for the U.S. taxpayer. We returned $485 million worth of supplies to the supply system by clearing forward operating bases of excess supplies. We provided water to five forward operating bases, and oversaw all ammunition coming into Iraq to support Coalition and Joint forces in Iraq and Afghanistan. We were selected to support training the Iraqi forces to improve their maintenance and supply capabilities, while rebuilding their civil capabilities. We also proved to the Active Component that the Army Reserve Sustainment Soldier was as good or better than they were. We created big and small events to share our time together; turning our plywood conference room into an epic Call-of-Duty game room on Fridays, celebrating birthdays, anniversaries and sports teams. We celebrated Christmas, New Years and

Easter.

We lost two fine, brave American Soldiers during our time there.

The 259th CSSB was awarded the Meritorious Unit Award for service in Operation Iraqi Freedom, and was deactivated from the Army inventory. My Soldiers and I returned home to an amazing Welcome Home ceremony at Ft Carson, Colorado, where we marched into the field house to Toby Keith's "American Soldier". We met our families after a year of separation. I honestly do not remember a lot about that formation. I just remember holding my children after more than 15 months away—and never wanting to let go. I remember feeling badly for those single Soldiers in my formation, or those whose families did not attend. And . . . I remember this bitter-sweet feeling of gratitude. We had made it!

Apparently, God knew what He was doing.

There are 350-something days of memories, of lessons, of things I wish I could do over, say over, handle differently, or just live again. There are memories I smile at, cringe at, and even cry about. There are faces or names I remember; and those I remember sometimes, and those I have forgotten but nevertheless impacted my memories, my success, and my failures during that year. We celebrated birthdays, marriages, births, and wins. We grieved the loss of two of our Soldiers, we mourned over divorces, over breakups, and of the year we lost from our families.

But here's what I know from that year....

1) No matter what, Lead Strong. Everyone is looking for leadership, and when you are placed in that privileged position, take it and lead with strength, purpose and compassion. Confidence does not come without taking the first step. It comes when you walk into your purpose. Your sense of worthiness is not something that you wait for, before your step. It is something that God reminds you of when you walk the path He lays before you.

2) Serve Selflessly. As I transition to my new adventures serving

organizations, assisting them to communicate and grow through change; it is not the medals, or recommendations that I treasure. My treasures are the moments that I made a difference in someone's life. It was the young Soldier that I challenged to organize the Battalion for the Joint Base Balad Olympics, and his delight when he accepted our trophy from the Commanding General on my behalf. It was the Soldiers that I walked with until they had the courage to seek support from the mental health professionals. It was standing with the team that serves behind the scenes in preparing our fallen Brothers and Sisters for their final trip home to their families, with dignity and honor, during our ramp ceremonies. It was watching former Sons of Iraq learn a new skill, and return with pride, and stories of their children. It was watching the 75 Army Reserve Soldiers stand tall and receive their Combat Patch, as one unit, one mission and one purpose.

3) Be Your Best Self. I was not sure that I was the right officer to take the 259th to war. I am sure there were plenty of others that were not sure either. But that didn't matter. I showed up. I lead strong. I gave my best. Some days were better than others, but I had a team that filled in my weaknesses, and supported my strengths. We showed up with our best stuff, everyday. It might be the Joint Base Balad Olympics' Lip Sync Competition where the leadership participated to raise the morale of the base. Or the conference room briefings that the staff learned, and grew, and became better at their profession; sometimes over their protests. It could also have been the moments in my office, where the Command Sergeant Major and I took turns telling ourselves not to react on emotion and to make the hard, best decision we could at the time.

4) Love Well. I am privileged to have had these adventures, and to live this life. None of it would have been possible without the love of my children, and the support of my family. These are the people we lean into, stand tall for, learn from and for… and love well. One friend recently reminded me that this is our purpose—Love Well. It makes all the other lessons learned possible.

Marci D. Toler

Marci D. Toler, LTC (Ret) is a combat veteran with several deployments under her belt. In addition to other awards and recognitions, she was awarded the Bronze Star for her meritorious efforts as the Commander, 259th Combat Sustainment Support Battalion. She is currently an author, speaker and CEO of Toler Leadership Consulting, partnering with corporate and faith-based organizations and leaders, improving their compassion and communications while harnessing the energy of change, to propel them forward and make a difference in the world. With over 33 years of public service, in the United States Army, she combines strategic thinking, compassion and value-based decision making to support leaders and organization in transition. Marci offers facilitated leadership coaching and workshops in leadership, value based decision making, value alignment and conflict resolution.

She is the Co-Founder of You Are Worthy Ministries, a non-denominational, non-profit Christian ministry that provides Christ-centered seminars and retreats for women focused on learning, understanding and accepting the truth of God's identity for each of us.

Marci is a proud graduate of Colorado State University in Business Economics, Econometrics and the RAM Battalion ROTC program. She went on to earn her Masters of Business Administration, Change Management, and was selected and graduated from the United States Senior Service College (US Army War College) with a Masters of Strategic Studies. She hopes to finish her PhD in Organization Management, when life slows down.

However, she is most proud that she is the mother of three children. They include Katherine, a Special Education Resource teacher; Geoffrey, a student of Agronomy at the University of Nebraska, Lincoln; and Joseph, who went home too soon.

Marci D. Toler
Toler Leadership Consulting
6211 Keith Road
Alliance, NE 69301
910-213-6467
Marci@TolerLeadershipConsulting.com

Irina Zlatogorova
Three Life Lessons

Hello, my name is Irina. My life story is just as different and unique as everybody else's. My bumpy, scary and exciting life journey took me to the highest level of purposeful living and self-realization that I've ever imagined. I attribute my personal achievement and success to the deepest fear of failure, not being good enough, not finding the real meaning of my life, and eventually, dying in obscurity. In this story, I would like to share my three biggest life lessons that helped me to overcome many obstacles and create the life I always wanted to have. I hope that by reading about my experiences, you will consider your life situation and think of the ways you can live your life fully with sheer passion, complete dedication and meaningful purpose.

Lesson #1—Invest in yourself and your education.

I thought that I won the lottery, when I arrived in the United States at the age of 20 from the Siberia region in Russia, the former Soviet Union. I wondered what I could accomplish in a foreign country, when I could not speak English, had no prior work experience and had not even finished my college education. I had no relatives, no friends and no money. Out of two jobs that I found at the beginning of my immigration, the first one was "for shelter" in exchange for house cleaning and gardening, and the second was minimum wage work in a grocery store. I struggled a lot, both emotionally and financially. However, I had high hopes for my future. I knew that to accomplish anything in this life, I had to invest in my education. Therefore, I started to study English and Accounting in a local community college. Ironically, despite my minuscule income, I was spending more money on school than on food during the first two years. Later, when I found a job as the Staff Accountant at a small manufacturing company, I enrolled in the accelerated bachelor degree program in 'Leadership and Management' at Judson University, a private Christian school in Elgin, Illinois. Luckily, my company paid for that education. As a result of the program, over time, I became a visible leader in my department and got promoted several times. However, I knew that I could do a lot more than counting the company's cash flow and decided to continue my education at Northern Illinois University. It was a fantastic move, since it helped me to find a higher paying job and become a team manager in a large corporation. When I received my Masters in Business Administration degree, I got promoted to a Director's role. I was only 33 years old!

Did I mention that I also had two kids both times when I went to school? That's right, as soon as I enrolled in each college program, I got pregnant! Therefore, I told both children that they already have college degrees, since my daughter went with me through the Bachelor's program; and my son finished an MBA by listening to all of the lectures and doing homework while being in my belly. When my fellow students would ask me about difficulties being pregnant, working full-time and going to school, I would joke and tell them that in my situation, I have a cognitive advantage since I've got two brains! However, in reality, it was very hard, and I promised myself that I would not go back to school until I was over 50, so there is no chance of me getting pregnant again.

Question: Can you get an additional education in your current situation?

Lesson #2 — 'Bad' situations can turn into 'Good' in the long run.

After the big promotion to the Director's position, my life was great, and I wanted to grow and learn even more. However, my husband (ex-husband now) did not feel the same way and openly discouraged my further self-development by being consistently negative and doubtful about my dreams and entrepreneurial business ideas. After two years of awful separation and inevitable divorce, I felt very lonely thinking that I fell below the lowest level of existence and started to question my life purpose. To cope with my daily misery and debilitating self-doubt, I desperately dived into self-help books and online courses on well-being. I then tried yoga and immediately fell in love with the practice. By reading volumes of inspirational books and doing yoga, I learned that feeling lonely and separate from others, is an illusion that causes pain and suffering to millions of people. In reality, we are all inseparable and dependent on one another. So, I started to meditate daily and ask myself questions about my soul such as: Who am I? What do I want to accomplish in this lifetime? How can I help and serve others? These "soul questions" were mentioned in several books on conscious living and self-discovery, so I kept repeating them to myself so that I would know the answers someday.

As a result of my self-inquiry, human psychology and interpersonal relationships became my new study interests. I learned how to read people's body language, their facial expressions and other non-verbal forms of communication. I became a better listener and more compassionate individual. I started to notice that people actively sought my company and attentively listened to my words of encouragement and advice. I began to formally and informally coach those individuals who went through some hardship and, just like me, were searching for their purpose in life. I loved to share my knowledge and experience when helping others and felt an immense joy, when I saw those people succeeding and thriving again.

Looking back, I realize that without the "bad" situation that I faced after my collapsed marriage, I would never have discovered my interests in yoga and behavioral psychology. I could never be as compassionate, understanding and helpful to others as I've become. In the long run, the "bad" situation turned into a "good" powerful experience, and I grew a lot. I'm now helping others to learn and grow by sharing this information. Yes, there is hope in every terrible situation.

Question: Do you have a 'bad' situation that you can turn around, thrive, and help others?

Lesson #3—Find out what is your passion.

Another benefit of having behavioral psychology knowledge was that I became an expert negotiator in procuring products and services at work and received numerous awards and recognitions for process improvements, building effective teams and encouraging teamwork. The peak of my career occurred when I was promoted to be VP of Procurement reporting to the company's CFO. As a department manager of over 100 people in the U.S. and overseas, I learned how to give assignments based on individuals' strongest skills and personal interests. I also started a "Yoga and Meditation" group through the company's social channel and became a formal mentor of many young women at the workplace through the Women in Leadership Development Network. I saw my mentees succeeding and getting promoted at a very high rate. Through coaching, mentorship, yoga, and meditation I realized there was one thing that I loved to do the most when dealing with people—I loved to TEACH!

Soon after the realization of my life purpose, my hunger for knowledge and education grew even stronger. I began searching for available doctorate programs with the goal of becoming a TEACHER (before turning 50!). The Northcentral University (NCU), an online college, had the most appealing Ph.D. in Business Administration program since it allowed me to combine my business experience and education in 'Leadership and Management', with my passion for human behavior and people interactions through the Industrial/Organizational (I/O) Psychology specialization. I was so eager to continue my education and deepen my knowledge of various work-life balance solutions through research and data that I decided to quit my highly prestigious and well-paid job in the company where I worked for the past fifteen years.

The reaction from people around me in response to my bold move was very surprising. Only a few people asked me if I lost my mind. Most of them said that they were envious of my decision and wished they could do the same thing. Unfortunately, many of them didn't even know what their real passion is! The advice to them was to keep asking the "soul questions" as frequently as possible until they got the answers. The way to know that the answers are true and real, is actually very simple—*feel them in your body*. When I first realized that my life purpose is to teach and that "I'm a teacher," my whole body responded with a sense of joy, warmth, and pleasure. It felt like a liquid honey flowed through my entire system, and my heart started to beat a little bit faster with excitement, almost if saying—"This is it! You got it!"

So, here is what I want:

I want to learn and teach others about the "well-being at a workplace." I imagine a future workforce that is driven by one common purpose—to succeed. I see people motivated to do things that they always wanted to do and achieve self-actualization. I believe that our world's health is highly dependent on the physical and mental health of individuals, including groups of people formed at various workplaces. My ultimate goal is to become a great educator, an innovator and a leader in the field of I/O Psychology.

Question: What is your passion?

Today, I live an authentic life that is full of excitement, new challenges and many wonders. In addition to my Ph.D. studies, I continue to do ad hoc business consulting work at various organizations on the topics of leadership, management and procurement processes. I also try to squeeze a few yoga-based stretches in between my training sessions with attendees, and they seem to enjoy the experience. I'm also working on becoming a certified yoga teacher and gaining a deeper understanding of yoga principles and yogic lifestyle. I even received a new spiritual name—Taran Vedya Kaur. 'Taran' in Sanskrit means a swimmer or a raft; 'Vedya' means knowledge or wisdom; 'Kaur' means the 'Lioness of God' who walks with grace and power. Every time someone calls me Taran Vedya Kaur, my soul is reminded of the destiny to ferry others across the material ocean of unconsciousness onto the shores of celestial awareness. Beautiful, isn't it?

Finally, I have a wonderful husband who supports my growth, wants to grow with me, and helps his clients to grow through effective motivational and coaching methods. Every day, we learn and share our new knowledge and experiences with each other. My kids are also doing very well. My daughter wants to have a career in the cyber security, and my son is interested in the medical science field. Both of them have told me that they are very proud of me. As I said before, my life has been bumpy, scary and exciting at the same time. I sincerely hope that the three life lessons about self-education, "bad" turning into "good" situations and personal passion discoveries in my story will help you to overcome your obstacles, stay focused on your life purpose, reach your highest goals and become your best self.

Irina Zlatogorova

Irina Zlatogorova is an independent business consultant with over 20 years of experience in leading and managing complex projects for Fortune 500 companies. She has demonstrated substantial process improvements and savings results in consumer products, home services, and the retail industry. Irina has been recognized for her expertise in effective contract negotiations, building teams, and providing mentorship to young business professionals.

In her previous role as a Divisional Vice President of Procurement for Sears Holdings Corporation, Irina was responsible for managing a team of 100 professionals and oversaw over $4 billion in annual spending for purchasing products and services. Her responsibilities included conducting supplier risk assessments, measuring team's performance against industry benchmarks, and providing continuing training to associates.

Before Procurement, Irina was a Compliance Officer for the Home Services organization at Sears. She was responsible for ISO 9000 standard implementation, as well as adherence to statutory and regulatory requirements for the service industry. She also has extensive experience with divestitures, mergers and acquisitions, business process outsourcing and spending analysis.

Irina is fluent in the English and Russian languages, has an MBA from Northern Illinois University and is pursuing her Ph.D. in Business Administration with specialization in Industrial Organizational Psychology from Northcentral University.

Irina Zlatogorova
902 Fox Chase Circle
St. Charles, IL 60174
630-945-4984
izshulman1@gmail.com

Svietlana Lavrentidi

It Was All Worth It

You probably heard that our personality and life depend on our childhood. I now know that it is true. I keep recognizing parts of me that are directly connected to my childhood. I see similar traits with other people too.

My message, character traits, fears, attitude, and behavior around other people, all started when I was little. It took me many years to discover these connections, identify where they are coming from and start transforming them into something positive. I know that one day I will look back and say, "It was all worth it"

It all started when I was very little, I used to witness my father beating my mom. Even though I loved my father more than anything or anyone in this world, I remember being scared to say anything. It was because I was afraid that he would hit me too. Mum says that once I actually did say to my dad "Dad, stop beating mom".

Thankfully, my mum left dad when I was 5. It was the right thing to do. However, I loved my father very much and I wanted to be with him. My crazy love was something that mom could never understand. She said she was even a bit jealous because he never did much, but I still loved him unconditionally. I know that there are still many things I do not know and mum refuses to tell me. She says that if she told me, I would never see him the same. However, the truth is that even today, no matter how bad it was and how terrible it was for my mother, I know I'd love him. This is true, even if he was a monster.

This affected my personal relationships very much later in life. I was a very happy child and I was pretty fearless. I wasn't afraid of anything, including pain. I could literally talk to anybody and I was always honest about what I said. I did get in trouble for telling strangers about things that were happening in my family.

It all changed one night. I didn't know it yet, I was still to find out...

"It's dark and it's cold. I'm alone and terrified. I have a gun in my little hands. We are shooting at each other. I cannot see who it is. But I feel this terrible pain in my chest. There is a huge rock next to me. I go hiding behind it. It's so big that it covers my little body. I am holding my chest... And then I look down at my hands, full of blood. I was shot. There is so much blood and so much pain... Why am I not dying...?" I woke up, still feeling the pain, still feeling like I was there. I was yet to find out why this dream was about to change me forever.

I cannot remember the timeline for the next events.

I remember someone calling the landline, my grandma picking up the phone and going pale. I heard that someone died. My grandma said to me that it was a distant relative. I did not believe her. I went to my room and started praying. "God please, please let it not be my father". I was crying and praying. But it was too late to pray... That night had changed me. I experienced my first and biggest loss. While losing my father, I lost my identity. However, I mainly lost my courage. I gained fear instead. It was fear of everything and everyone. There was also fear of people, fear of speaking and fear of trusting myself.

The rest of my childhood was a torture. I was bullied in schools. I was not able to answer in my lessons. I was continuously scared. Even when I knew the right answer, I was still afraid to be wrong, so I said nothing because I was scared to be laughed at.

My grandma always said when I grow up, I'll look back missing those years since they are the best years. She was so wrong. I hated my childhood. There was nothing there to miss. Those years brought my biggest loss, pain and fear.

There was only one thing that I absolutely loved. I discovered music. I loved singing. My dream was to become a singer. I was in the school choir and then in the school band. This was the only happy place I had. I wanted to learn to play the piano, but my grandparents refused. I wanted to be a singer, but my grandma said: "It's a dirty business and you'll have to sleep with everyone. You will not be a singer". I had no support for my dream. How could I believe that I could go after my dream, when my family didn't believe that I was good enough?

My mother had to travel and make a living. I hardly saw her. She did her very best to provide and to secure a much better future for me than she ever had. I was with my grandparents for several years. The night I lost my dad, was the night I lost my ability to trust myself enough and to fight for my dreams. I needed someone to tell me that I could and should do it. But there was nobody around me to guide me, to encourage me, to support me... There was nothing for me in that life anymore.

In 2003, my mum came to London in the United Kingdom. It was my dream to live in this beautiful city. I don't know why. I just wanted it so much. Mum brought me to visit and I begged her to stay. I instantly fell in love with London. It was the first time in my life that I felt at home. I cannot explain why, but it just seemed right. I will forever be grateful to my mum for making that dream come true. This was the time when "luck" started finding me. It was time for change. It was time to find my identity and to work towards becoming myself again.

There were many challenges, but I started to rediscover who I was and why I was here. I went through excitement and disappointment.

There were good times, such as first love, first job, being accepted to one of the top colleges in the arts, getting better jobs, parties, learning experiences, etc.

But there were also challenging times including: suicidal thoughts, betrayal, nervous breakdowns, weakness and fatigue and an inability to be there for myself or others.

It all shaped me. It gave me a new perspective and new understandings. It took me a long time to build up my confidence. I had to learn to accept myself for who I am and not who family wants me to be. I had to start making my own "mistakes". They were the ones I wanted to make and the ones I wanted to live through. I can honestly say that I do not regret any of them. I received a lot of judgement from people I love. It was not because I did something wrong, as **there is no right and wrong, there just IS**, it was because our understanding of life was very different... Life is about making our own choices, our own mistakes and fighting our own battles. It's only personal with ourselves, not with others. Our family and friends can take our actions personally, but it isn't. We all deserve to follow our own paths.

In 2012–2013, my entrepreneurial journey began. I discovered personal development. I discovered a new world that is full of opportunities. It is where I can be me and where I am finally accepted. I started Entrepreneurial Women's Network which I grew to be the largest female Meetup in Europe in just 6 months. I discovered public speaking. I was invited to share my skills and my story with other people. I have met some incredible people through networking and from this I have started a daily podcast show "Entrepreneurcast", where I interview some of the best entrepreneurs of our time.

My journey is still developing over time and my story is not over. I am doing what I am doing, because I know there are people out there who have gone through challenges and have struggled to get back up. There are people who are facing their battles daily. They sometimes feel that it is easier to just end it. There are people in so much pain, that they are trying to suppress their pain in any way possible. This includes medications, drugs, alcohol or physical pain. I know that sometimes our emotional pain gets to the level when physical pain feels like a joy. This is because it helps to numb our emotions, since it helps to distract us and feel better for a short while. I know you are out there. I know that I can feel your pain, because I felt it, I am still feeling it. I want you to know that you are not alone. You can pull through and you can change your life for the better. **YOU ARE AMAZING, YOU ARE BEAUTIFUL AND YOU ARE UNIQUE. STAY YOU. I LOVE YOU.**

Before I end this chapter, I want to share my vision with you. I want to share why I am grateful. I now know what I lived through was for a reason. I am here to help and serve. I also have a mission. My mission is to change the way the world works. I want to change the lives of the future generations. I have discovered what I am here to do. Trust me, there is a plan for all of us. We just have to be willing to find out.

I came into this life to live through my childhood challenges and traumas in order to prevent other kids from going down the same paths, wherever it can be done. I am now grateful for those experiences, because I can understand what others are going through.

Everything I do is building towards starting my charity, for the children of the future, children with vision and children on a mission.

Imagine if every child was raised, nurtured, given education, support and knowledge in exactly what they want to do. There would be no judgement and they could do whatever they wanted to. If a kid wants to be a teacher, why not? Dancer, gardener, fire fighter, astronaut, writer, builder, business owner, why not?

Our parents do their best to protect us and do what they think is right for us. But in doing that, they can end up killing our dreams. Because they think they know what's best or better for us. I disagree. They lived through their pains, challenges and losses, still that should not stop us from living ours.

We all deserve to follow our hearts. What if every child was given this choice, but also had help to discover what his/her strengths and gifts are the possibilities for growth, what is out there and how to get there? What if their schools were paid for and they had support and encouragement every step of the way?

Do you think that these kids when they grow up would take drugs, abuse alcohol or commit crimes? I don't think so. Why would they, if they follow their passion? What if they discovered personal development from a very young age? What if they knew how to develop good relationships and what to do in order to build a strong loving family? Don't you think that wars would be over? Corruption would disappear? Poverty would be gone? This would require huge amounts of funds, strength and courage. However, if the world could become a better place, wouldn't it be worth it? I believe it is.

Today this is one woman's vision, but one day I believe it will grow and build into something beautiful.

I was always told that I am naïve and a dreamer, who lives in a non-existent world. Maybe it is true and maybe I believe in the impossible, but as we know IMPOSSIBLE=I M POSSIBLE.

When I was little, my dreams were murdered, just like my father was. But *I grew into a courageous woman and I am the only person who can decide which of my dreams live*. While I am alive, I will fight for my dreams until my very last breath. I encourage you to do the same. **STAY STRONG, STAY COURAGEOUS AND STAY FEARLESS. STAY YOU. I LOVE YOU.**

Svietlana Lavrentidi

Svietlana is proof that nothing is impossible. She had her share of challenges, had several breakthroughs and overcame every obstacle on her path to success. Svietlana has discovered her past connected to her present and has been working on turning the connection into a positive ever since.

After having a stress related breakdown at work, she realized she was not cut out to be an employee and set out on a journey to become an entrepreneur.

After a couple of failed attempts, she found the keys to success and started her first successful business with NO funding and NO money. Within 6 months, she had built the largest female meetup group in Europe, which led her to becoming the authority in the world of meetups, networking and female entrepreneurship.

She is now inspiring entrepreneurs all over the UK and teaching them how to influence with ease, network effectively and get to their dreams faster, by becoming The Authority Ninja in your field.

Svietlana also has a bigger vision for everything she does.

Want to know more? Get in touch now and remember to register for a VIP list.

Svietlana Lavrentidi
The Authority Ninja
00447973558831
sl@svietlana.com
theauthorityninja.com
theentrepreneurcast.com
svietlana.com
entrepreneurialwomensnetwork.com

Michele Riley Swiderski

Navigating Life Part Two…Let It Go

When I was young, many of my friends called me "Princess". OK. Truth be told, most still do. This wasn't due to porcelain skin, dwelling in a castle or having handsome men offer me glass shoes following events. It was simply a way of being. It was a thought process in which I believed that if I followed societal guidelines and questioned only things I believed to be unjust, everything would work out for me in the end. I believed in this wholeheartedly. I thought, of course, society, the universe and God have rules of engagement and if I follow them, the forces will align to make me happy and successful.

Therefore, I diligently took steps to insure that the forces would align in my favor in the future. I took advanced classes in high school, graduated early and began college classes at just sixteen. Some stumbling blocks and injuries while in college, only strengthened my resolve. I refocused my efforts to stay on the prescribed path. While in college and working part-time, I met Peter, the older man I was to marry. We married right after I graduated from college with a double major. I felt that I was ahead of the curve again. I was happily married, thus being promoted from princess to queen, living in a beautiful home and looking forward to starting our family at only twenty-two.

As the years passed, the princess aura continued. I, along with everyone else, believed that I was living a charmed life. I was a happy mother of two, working in my own small business marketing firm, volunteering at the children's private school and our church, helping out at the family business and enjoying the comfortable life we had made. But we weren't able to stay "comfortable" indefinitely. Economic times being what they were and what they still are, our family business began to struggle. Even a strong business, which was a leader in its field with a fifty-five year history, couldn't withstand the economic downturn and had to ultimately close its doors.

Stress became a normal operating model during the eighteen months it took my husband, Peter, to find and accept a comparable position. It began to overwhelm him, since he felt it necessary to keep the details of our financial struggles from me. I could see the changes in him. While there were celebrations when he returned to the workforce with a prominent new position, he was nearly fifty and beginning a new career path. His blood pressure began to climb, as did his weight. He developed diabetes and cholesterol issues. I couldn't let his health continue to deteriorate, without taking some of the burden off of him. I began to seriously consider the marketing and public relations offers I had been receiving. I ultimately closed my one-woman shop and accepted a position from an old friend with a manufacturing/operations organization within a large government defense contractor in visitor logistics and event management.

I took on my new position with a whistle-while–you-work attitude. I grew the position and grew along with the position. I felt that I had created a valuable niche position and managed to keep school hours to allow me to still manage my family effectively. I (along with others) felt that I was charming my way through adversity.

The tide had finally turned. With two full-time incomes, we finally began to save money again and plan for glorious, fun-filled family vacations. However, somehow that dreaded eighteen month mark was problematic for us again. With only a year and a half under my belt at my new corporate position, I received a phone call which could only be given justice by the Disney music "DU DU DUN". The rest of that fateful day was akin to the tornado from the Wizard of Oz. I was receiving information from a variety of sources, but none of it made any sense. I followed the instructions I received. How could I not, being who I was? I made my way from my suburban Chicago office to

Northwestern University Hospital downtown.

I was greeted by Peter's administrative assistant, who took me directly to a nurse, who in turn, took me to a private room. I was panicked, annoyed, tired and most of all frustrated. Suddenly, I just wanted to see the "man behind the curtain" who presumably had all the answers and could end all of this chaos. I came to find out that there were three men behind the curtain, as a senior physician, counselor and priest entered the small room.

To this day, I don't know exactly what was said to me. All I could think was, "I was told he was having trouble breathing". I was in a definite poppy field fog! The priest laid his hand on my shoulder, but I couldn't move. He then placed a hand on each side of my face and looked directly at me and said, "Did you hear the doctor? Peter did not survive the ambulance ride to the hospital." What?!? I thought didn't survive what? I must have had a non-responsive look on my face, as the doctor repeated, "Mrs. Swiderski, Peter suffered a massive heart attack. We did everything in our power to save him, but we were not successful." The daze of the poppy field took over again. I felt like I was suffocating and needed fresh air. The priest again placed his hand on my shoulder and said, "Listen to me young lady. You have some important decisions to make. It is moments like these which define who you are and who you are to become. Now, who would you like us to call?"

I wept through traumatic calls to my neighbor, my brother and Peter's brother. The Tin Man-like doctor retuned to the room with the nurse. They began asking about organ donation, saying there was an immediate need. I was thinking that this man has absolutely no heart. I remember the doctor saying it was my decision, that there had been a motorcycle accident and the patient was in immediate need upstairs. I replied that I would need to think about it. The Tin Man told me I had twenty minutes.

Twenty minutes later, with my tiara firmly positioned on my head, I donated nearly 50 percent of Peter's body; skin, organs, eyes, bones, and marrow. I had originally said no to the bones because we have children and there would be an open casket. However, the counselor had found a donor to create prosthetics for his limbs for the funeral services.

The nurse finally returned and asked if I wanted to see Peter before he went into the donation procedures. By that time, our brothers were arriving and we asked for the sequence of events. Peter had suffered a sudden and severe heart attack shortly after arriving at work on the 38th floor of his downtown office building. Heroic measures were taken to get him to the ambulance and treat him, but he passed away prior to reaching the hospital. I wanted to believe the location of his office on the 38th floor, the city, the traffic; his company and the lack of a defibrillator were all to blame. However, it was ultimately the stress and overwhelm of the previous years which had taken an irreversible toll on his body. It had created a tornado for us with the house landing on my husband and not the wicked witch.

I wailed in the room with my lifeless life partner. When our brothers approached the gurney, I anticipated more wailing, but there was only silent misery. I continued to wail for the next few days, at society, the universe, God and even Disney the creator of modern day fairy tales. I had followed the rules laid out for me and this was my reward? I was suddenly widowed in my 30's with two children in grade school. "Where is MY happily ever after?" I shouted!

The priest was correct. It is in moments like those that you begin to define what your future will look like. In the days and weeks which followed, I adjusted my tiara but refused to dull the sparkle. Grief counselors led me to believe that because the children had already suffered such a sudden and tragic loss, as much of their lives as possible should remain the same. Where is that fairy God Mother when you most need her? Keeping the status quo meant making the payment in an overly mortgaged home, private school and club sports. Therefore, I did what any girl who was just demoted from Queen to Princess would do. I put on my big girl pants, went back to work and applied for a promotion and raise. I secured the promotion, kept the status quo, began working on my MBA, and kept busy raising seemingly happy, healthy, well-adjusted, bright children.

No problem, right? Except for one thing. I had recreated the stress and overwhelm my husband experienced. My children and I were failing and we didn't even know it. On the outside, we looked like the perfect picture of recovery. This is just how I had designed my storybook to appear to those on the outside looking in. But on the inside, after years of keeping up this pace, the children and I had begun to suffer from autoimmune disorders, adrenal fatigue, asthma, allergies and heart issues.

It took years for me to realize how much stress we were taking on and the severity of the problems it was creating. By the time the children reached high school, they were taking advanced classes, participating in club and high school sports and working part-time. I was pursuing an advanced degree, volunteering, attending all their activities and working 45+ hours per week.

At the suggestion of a friend, I began attending yoga and meditation classes. This created a change in perspective that I had not expected. I had anticipated learning how to stretch and eliminate my stress and stiffness. However, I was drawn into a totally different mindset. I attended more workshops and classes and was eventually introduced to a holistic nutritionist. My brain actually began to change shape! What seemed so important before, now could only be considered in the context of my well-being and the well-being of my children. We could not be effective participants in society and truly successful, if we were not well from within.

Things in our world slowly began to change. I met Dan, who would become my partner for life, part two. He is a man who is wellness conscious, grows his own food, enjoys the simple pleasures of life and runs his own small remodeling firm. I began to give thoughtful consideration to not only what we ate, but where it came from, how it would benefit us and where and how we ate it. I began to build buffers into our continually time-compressed, achievement oriented schedules. I walked and did aerobics while the children were at their athletic practices. We eliminated soda, gluten and dairy from our diets, as much as possible. We felt better, but were still not truly well.

I finally realized that wellness is not an occasional thing. I began to learn more about core wellness and other holistic practices. We started a garden, had acupuncture and chiropractic treatments and I began to learn about the benefits of therapeutic grade essential oils. Through learning advanced meditation techniques, deep reflection and the regular use of essential oils, I came to determine that I needed to return to my entrepreneurial roots. I, therefore, began a holistic wellness business as my small way of breaking the cycle of what I now call self-inflicted achievement illnesses.

In 2016, I began Simply Balanced with Michele, a provider of natural wellness solutions for health and home through the proper use of therapeutic grade essential oils, natural foods and education. This firm was founded on the resolve to embrace the second part of life with a holistic outlook, the strength of a lasting love with my significant other, Dan, and the support of my fellow holistic practitioners who helped to provide the information and strength to return to my roots. In doing so, I "let go" of the frozen, stagnant ideals of traditional ideas regarding success. By adding lavender plants to my tiara, I am able to make positive, impactful changes for my family, my relationship and all who enter my circle through business or friendship.

Michele Riley Swiderski

Michele Swiderski is a Natural Solutions provider who helps women become healers in their own homes. A mom with two small children who was suddenly widowed in her 30's, Michele began her wellness firm, Simply Balanced with Michele, to share her lessons learned from overcoming the stress of suddenly single parenting, a more than 40 hour per week corporate position and the community commitments that she was drawn toward.

Michele's journey is one of joyful resilience. Prior to founding her wellness business, Michele spent over 10 years as a visitor logistics and military event planner for a large government defense contractor. Before that, she established herself as a small business marketing consultant.

Michele is now creating a movement assisting her clients as they embrace wellness through the proper use of therapeutic grade essential oils, natural foods and education. She was called to this work through the experience of autoimmune issues, which she and her children experienced from grief, chronic stress and overwhelm. Michele provides services including one-on-one wellness coaching, in-home classes, seminars for other holistic wellness practitioners and their clients and entrepreneurial coaching.

Michele holds a double bachelor's degree in Marketing Communications and Public Relations with an emphasis in Entrepreneurial Business. She is currently finishing her MBA. She enjoys participating in a wide variety of wellness activities, yoga, meditation, reiki, chiropractic care and acupuncture. Michelle also collaborates with other holistic wellness practitioners.

"I receive tremendous satisfaction and joy from helping people to find natural wellness solutions for health and home in simple, obtainable ways. Living well and incorporating daily wellness routines can change everything about how you live and the way your family functions."

Michele Riley Swiderski
Simply Balanced with Michele
St. Charles, IL 60174
847-727-4962
SimplyBalancedMichele@yahoo.com
SimplyBalancedwithMichele.com

La Tanya D. Hinton

When the Smoke Clears

Think of a behavior pattern that is acquired by frequent repetition. It could be good or bad. When it is bad, is becomes what most of us are in denial of. It is a habit. There are many habits that can play role in various facets of our lives. My bad habits were practiced late in life in comparison to my peers. It was a lesson that was learned many times. You should compare yourself to no one else and follow your own path. It was after I graduated from high school that I indulged in drinking alcohol and smoking marijuana. I would smoke marijuana wrapped in cigar papers with my friends and associates. At first, it was once in a while for recreational usage. In my magnificent, magical, magnifying mind, I thought I wouldn't be affected by the consequences of my actions. As time went on, when I didn't have marijuana, I would buy cigars to smoke. The cigars came four in a pack. I would smoke all of the cigars in one day. My friends noticed that my once in a while recreational fun had turned into an addiction. It was suggested that I indulge in my addiction a lot slower than I had previously done. I then went and did the next addicting thing. I bought a package of cigarettes and began smoking them at a rate of one package per day. This began around the age of 21. While I made multiple attempts to quit on my own, my attempts failed. There would be many times where I would chain smoke while at work. My lunch break would be a half an hour. I ate but I also made it a priority to smoke at least two cigarettes within that time frame.

Since 1994, I have worked as a Certified Nursing Assistant in different capacities. I have gotten great pleasure from assisting others who need help with doing what a lot of us take for granted every day. Other habits that I had acquired were not setting boundaries and suppressing my thoughts and feelings. I took care of everyone else's needs, while mine went lacking most of the time. I did not utilize any productive or fruitful outlets.

A DEEPER RELATIONSHIP

As a child, it was not impressed upon me to go to church, unless I was with my neighbors or my grandparents. I had gotten baptized by water at the age of 19. However, I didn't truly start taking my relationship with God seriously until the age of 26. I found myself feeling like I was at home at a small church in Bellwood, Illinois. I became familiar with the members, just as they became familiar with me. I served as a member, a choir member and a Sunday school teacher.

HOLDING IT ALL IN

On Thanksgiving Day 2011, my best friend committed suicide. In December of that same year, I lost another close friend, and in January 2012, I lost a distant cousin. Those losses affected me to the point where I was barely functioning. I didn't know how to handle things. Instead of leaning on God during that time, I unconsciously made attempts to handle it all on my own. I became numb, internalized it all, and began drinking more alcohol and smoking more cigarettes. It wasn't until 2015 and 2016, that I began to release what had been festering for a long time. I had become angry and unforgiving with God, myself and others. I went through long periods of depression and isolation. Every day that passed, I was dying on the inside. It wasn't until I started being more committed to my relationship with God that my life started to slowly change. I was invited by one of the associate ministers to participate in several spiritual gatherings and exercises. This involved abandoning my old ways of doing things and adopting new ways of thinking and living. I was being pushed into my purpose. Some of the exercises included creating a vision board as well as writing a paper on the women in the Bible. Participating in these things helped me to dig deep down and to clean up the things that I had been internalizing for many years.

Even though I had a relationship with God, I longed for more intimacy. While my sleep pattern had been disturbed, it gave me many opportunities to have a deeper relationship with God. I took them joyfully! I found myself waking up at what initially seemed like odd times of the morning. Some days I would wake up at 2:30 am, while other times it would be 3:30 am. No matter the time, I looked forward to getting into the presence of God. I enjoyed praying, reading the Bible and working towards getting a better understanding of how to study the Scriptures effectively.

I had taken a Kingdom Class, where I was educated on how I play a part in God's big plan. I learned about how every person that God created, was born with special gifts and abilities. I also learned that God will use everything that we go through to help someone else. He lines up the right people at the right places at the right times with the right things. The class was taught by an awesome woman of God who is very in tune with her spirituality; she became my friend, Spiritual Mother and mentor.

On March 9, in a Facebook message, she asked me to pray for cancer survivors. I met the request as best as I knew how.

A BUMP ALONG THE ROAD

In March 2016, I found a lump in my breast while I was doing a breast self-exam. As I touched the lump, I felt a stinging sensation. I became concerned and made preparations to call my primary care physician. When I called to schedule an appointment, I was told that the doctor had no available appointments until the following month. I immediately thanked the person on the other end of the phone and hung up. I then dialed the telephone number of my gynecologist. I explained my recent findings and was scheduled for an appointment within a few hours. While I was relieved to get into the doctor's office the same day as making the appointment, my mind began going through an anxious process. I had done a breast self-exam many years earlier and had a mammogram because I found a lump. The results found that the lump was benign. As I drove to the appointment and sat in the waiting area, all I could hear were words being rehearsed in my mind that said, "You will need to have a mammogram done." I then began to wonder how long it would take before the nurse and doctor would see me. I waited a short time before my name was called. I was escorted and prepped for the doctor within 10 minutes. Before I could hear all of the "What if" questions pop up in my head, the doctor entered the room and examined me. He said that I would be given a written order for a mammogram and that I was to call and make an appointment as soon as possible. The next business day, I called and scheduled a mammogram appointment for March 23. On the days leading up to the appointment, I did my best to stay focused and carry on with my regular routine.

On the day of the mammogram, I was truly being tested. I got there on time, registered and then sat down. I heard many names being called. However, my name was not mentioned. I waited about an hour, before I went to see what was taking so long. It turned out that even though I was registered, somehow my name got crossed off the sign in sheet and I was missed. After getting that rectified, I was seen immediately. I went through the formal paperwork and while doing so, I paid very close attention to the customer service representative. She made it a point to show compassion while assisting me. She used comforting words to let me know that there was nothing to worry about and not to be fearful of anything. My response to the hour wait, along with the representative's soothing words, were confirmation that God was definitely around. Once I was escorted to the changing room and changed clothes, it didn't take long before I was taken to have the mammogram. The technician was very confident and reassuring about what would take place during the mammogram. She expressed that whatever the outcome was, I would be notified by my doctor. The technician did a very thorough job. Before I could leave, a doctor came to tell me to schedule a breast biopsy.

THE BREAST BIOPSY

The biopsy was scheduled for March 28. The breast biopsy came with its own set of preconceived thoughts. I had not experienced one before and just the idea of skin being taken away from me was scary. After the doctor took the time to explain to me what was to take place ahead of time, my fear diminished. The whole process was not as painful as I initially thought. I was once again told that my gynecologist would contact me with my results.

On March 29, I received a phone call stating that I had stage 0 DCIS, also known as the beginning stages of ductal carcinoma in-situ breast cancer. It was suggested that I get in contact with a surgeon to further discuss what could be done about the findings. Believe it or not, after hanging up the phone, I was in shock. Tears rolled down my face. I cried for a few seconds, wiped my face and collected myself. I texted my Spiritual Mother the diagnosis that the doctor gave. She called me immediately. I told her about what took place. She began to tell me how I would be contacting my sister-in-law for assistance. I texted my sister-in-law to tell her of the doctor's diagnosis. She asked if I had any plans. My response was, "To stop smoking." I asked her, "What do you suggest?" She responded by saying that she has resources. My sister-in-law had gone through the grueling and painful experience of being diagnosed with Celiac Disease. It is an immune response reaction to eating gluten, a protein found in wheat. It has over 300 different symptoms; one being cancer. From that point forward, my whole life changed.

MY LIFE STYLE CHANGE

My sister-in-law showed me how to heal my body. I began getting rid of all the food that I had in my kitchen. Starting the first week in April and for 21 days, I did a detoxification. I changed my eating habits along with what I ate. The purpose was to heal and restore the damaged cells in my body. It was a lifestyle change. With fresh fruits and vegetables, natural herbs and spices and the right foods and supplements, I would be healed. What was so special about this situation? I would not be having chemotherapy or radiation.

During the visits with the surgeon, he explained how I would have a panel of doctors that would be assisting me through my process. The surgeon and the oncologist suggested the conventional treatment methods of treating cancer which consists of surgery, chemotherapy and radiation.

I chose to also have surgery to keep up with my new lifestyle change. I was scheduled to have a mastectomy. My skin became radiant and I lost 30 pounds within a month and a half. By the time I was scheduled to have surgery, my cells had already begun to repair themselves and the tumor had shrunk. I had amazing considerable support from my biological and Spiritual family and friends. There were many people who came to sit with me before and after the surgery. The anesthesiologist said that the room had hit capacity. After taking some time to initially heal, I had post-surgery appointments. All of the follow-up appointments have confirmed that I am cancer free. I am a cancer conqueror. I am in high hopes of giving to others what was given to me, the gifts of forgiveness, love, life, letting go, and healing.

La Tanya D. Hinton

La Tanya D. Hinton is a Daughter of The Most High God, a Certified Nursing Assistant, Sunday school teacher, aspiring poet, spoken word artist and a cancer conqueror. She delights in being a servant for God. She has worked as a Certified Nursing Assistant in various health institutions in the mid-western states of Indiana, Wisconsin, Minnesota and Illinois. While she has received much joy in assisting the elderly in different nursing homes, her greatest satisfaction has consisted of working with medically fragile special needs children with cerebral palsy. La Tanya has also assisted in ministry work for the less fortunate.

La Tanya D. Hinton
708-971-5001
tanyad2002@yahoo.com

Danielle Di Cosola

My Rock Bottom Blessing

"I deeply resonate with the Phoenix in that I rose from the darkness and ashes to become a more vibrant, stronger, beautiful version of my former self." —Danielle Di Cosola

When people meet me and interact with me, they describe me as a confident, outgoing, funny, intellectual woman with a great head on her shoulders. People have naturally gravitated towards me because of my personality, how I treat them and the amount of positivity that I give off. I strive to be a good person, inside and out. What people don't know is that I have not always been that positive optimistic lady. There was a point in time where I was the exact opposite. But as my quote states, I rose from the darkness and ashes to become a stronger, more vibrant and beautiful version of my former self.

For a long time I struggled with depression, self-image, self-esteem and anxiety. A lot of what I was feeling stemmed from my family life. I was the only child that my mother and father had together. Because of some bad blood, I grew up without knowing my biological dad. My main father figure was my grandfather and I also had my step-father. My relationship with my mother was rocky. I now know that it was because we were way more alike than we were different. We both have very strong personalities and we clashed a lot. Since I didn't know anything about my biological father as I was growing up, I always felt like there was something missing. I didn't have a true sense of who I really was. Even though my stepfather's family was always good to me and treated me like I was their own, I still felt that something was missing and I would never really fit in or belong. There was also a huge gap in communication between me and my mother. I didn't want to make her upset with me and I didn't feel like she would really understand what I was feeling. She had always known and had a relationship with her birth mother and father, so how could she possibly understand what it was like not knowing your birth father.

As I progressed into my teenage years, my struggles with depression, self-image, self-esteem and anxiety became more of a burden. I always compared myself to other people. When I looked in the mirror, I saw this ugly girl who was never going to be good enough. I didn't love myself at all. My view of myself was always negative. I would often look at other people and wonder why I couldn't be as pretty, or as smart as they were. I thought that everyone around me had it better than me in some way, shape or form. My mom and I continued to clash because I felt like she was too strict and never let me do anything. It wasn't until I became a mother myself, that I understood why she was the way that she was. It helped me to comprehend the motive behind her actions. In addition, I felt like I could never be honest with her about anything because it would end up in a fight. As a result, I kept a lot of things to myself. I also made several questionable decisions that would get me into trouble and I was engaging in activities that were detrimental to my physical and mental health. I didn't know it at the time, but I was headed down a very dark path within myself.

When I finished high school, I chose to move away to go to college. The only reason that I chose to move away, was to get away from my family. I felt like they would never understand me and now they were too far away to tell me what to do. What I didn't realize was that I was not mature enough to handle that type of independence. I figured that the farther away I moved, the farther away I would be from the issues that I always struggled with. I didn't grasp the concept that I needed to face those issues and work on them or order for them not to control me anymore. While I was away, I got into drinking and drug use. I was falling deeper and deeper into the darkness. Drinking and doing drugs was an escape. I didn't think about how much my negative emotions were consuming me. I would soon get to the point where I was numb. On the outside, I was the girl who was always up for anything and loved to party and have fun. On the inside, I was very lost and hurt. I was getting to the point of convincing myself that I would be better off dead than alive. Those demons that I always struggled with ruled me and had complete control of me. My outlook on life was bleak and my thoughts of being truly happy were non-existent. All of this would soon become too overwhelming and lead me into the night that changed my life forever.

I was in my dorm room. I had just had a fight with my boyfriend at the time. I was still having issues with my family, even though they were far away. After having a panic attack, I made the decision that I was tired of living. I was tired of trying to fight the demons and I was done. It was time to throw in the towel. I didn't want to live this life anymore. At the age of 19, I attempted suicide. I locked myself in the bathroom of my dorm room and downed 20 Nyquil gel caps and 20 Benadryl pills. I came out of the bathroom and lay down on my bed. My roommate at the time knew something was wrong but she didn't know what I did. I just told her I was fine and tried to drift off to sleep hoping to never wake up. I was not able to fall asleep and I started acting weird. It almost felt like I was flying. My roommate knew something was wrong, so she alerted the Resident Advisor and they took me to the ER. I was then taken to a room, where I was surrounded by doctors and nurses. There was a point where I could no longer hear what was going on around me. I could see them moving fast but I could not hear anything that they were saying. I then looked to the far end of the room where there was a door. The door opened and a man in a white suit walked in. It was the most pure version of white I had ever seen in my life. He didn't walk over to me and he didn't say anything to me. He just looked me in the eye, lifted up his finger and waved it side to side. I really believe that was God sending an angel to tell me that it wasn't my time yet. After he did that, he walked out the door. I could hear the doctors and nurses say that I had been stabilized. It turned out that when I was experiencing divine intervention, I was on the verge on having a major heart attack due to the amount of prescription drugs I had put into my body. They had to give me steroids to slow down my heart and pump my stomach. I should have died that day, but God gave me a second chance.

The first night that I was in the hospital, I just kept wondering why. Why didn't I just die? Why was God giving me a second chance? All I could do was cry because I was so confused. There was lady sitting in the room with me because I was considered a danger to myself and needed supervision. She saw me crying and just told me that I would get through this and I would be OK. I was then transferred to an inpatient unit, where my family came to see me. I was so embarrassed. How could I ever look them in the eye again, let alone look myself in the eye? My family requested that I be transferred to a unit closer to home and I agreed. I was an inpatient for five days where I was monitored day and night. I had a lot of time to think. How was I going to move on from this and did I have the strength to do it? I was then presented with the opportunity to participate in a day program where I would receive intensive group therapy, individual counseling and other methods of treatment. I was really nervous about it. However, it was the best decision that I ever made for myself. There I was able to get the help that I needed to help myself and to heal. For the first time, I faced myself and was honest with myself. It was difficult and frightening at first, but in doing so, I was enlightened and allowed myself to begin to heal. When I did that, the old me had started to fade away and the new me began to make her debut. I started the process of learning to love myself and gain the strength and confidence to better myself. Once I got to the point of being comfortable with myself, I was able to mend my relationships with my family. Once I started to love myself, I had the capacity to let others love me as well.

I can honestly say that the road to my recovery was not an easy one. It took a lot of hard work, perseverance and lessons learned to get to the point I am at today. I still keep working at it and moving forward. I have learned that beauty encompasses so much more than just physical appearance. That beauty is truly in the eyes of the beholder and that YOUR EYES have to see it in yourself first before anyone else can. I learned that once you can honestly and wholeheartedly face yourself, you can face ANYONE and accomplish ANYTHING! I learned that we are our own worst critic and our own best cheerleader. You have to continually make a solid effort to empower the cheerleader and not the critic. I learned that you have to let go and make peace with the past, in order to move confidently and lovingly into your future.

I thank God for giving me a second chance. Had he not given me a second chance, I would have never experienced what true love is with my husband, the love of being a mother and being able to enjoy my relationships with my family and friends. I believe that God gave me a second chance not only for me to build myself up, but to help others in similar situations do the same. I hope that this story will inspire you to love yourself no matter what and incorporate the lessons that I have learned in your own life. Know and BELIEVE that you are good enough and strong enough to get up when you fall, dust yourself off and keep improving yourself. You are worth it and you deserve to be happy!

I still struggle with depression and anxiety from time to time, but I know how to cope with it and not let it consume me. I have been able to identify what I call my "Series of Events", so I know what help I need in order to keep moving forward and loving and believing in myself. I promised myself that I would never allow myself to fall that deep ever again. I have too much to live for and truly believe that the best is yet to come.

Danielle Di Cosola

Danielle Di Cosola is a Real Estate Broker for Coldwell Banker Residential Brokerage, located in Schaumburg, IL. Danielle is originally from Chicago, where she graduated from Robert Morris University with a BA in Business Management. Before venturing into the world of real estate, Danielle worked in the corporate sector, focusing on roles in the areas of sales, customer service, and human resources. She brings a wealth of knowledge on how to best service her clients from her experiences in those fields.

Since joining Coldwell Banker, Danielle has prided herself in her enthusiastic and genuine interest to deliver the results requested from her clients. She is committed to finding the perfect fit, whether you are listing, buying or renting a home.

In her free time, Danielle enjoys creating memories with her husband of

10 years and their two beautiful children. A friend of many, she loves embarking on entrepreneurial ventures, cooking, entertaining friends and family, reading, creating crafty items and relishing in the joy of helping others! Her family and friends describe her as an outgoing, loving and loyal person with an optimistic can-do attitude.

Danielle Di Cosola
Coldwell Banker Residential Brokerage- Schaumburg
20 N. Roselle Rd
Schaumburg, IL 60193
847-250-7277
Danielle.DiCosola@cbexchange.com
www.DanielleDiCosola.cbintouch.com

Jennifer Pestikas

Keep Moving Forward

"Let me tell you something you already know. The world ain't all sunshine and rainbows. It's a very mean and nasty place and I don't care how tough you are it will beat you to your knees and keep you there permanently if you let it. You, me, or nobody is gonna hit as hard as life. But it ain't about how hard you hit. It's about how hard you can get hit and keep moving forward. How much you can take and keep moving forward. That's how winning is done!"

—Sylvester Stallone, Rocky Balboa

You're not qualified. You don't have what it takes. You can't do that. Who do you think you are? You're not enough. How many times have you heard this in your life and your career? And more importantly, how many times have you believed this voice, whether it was from someone else or inside your own head?

Over the years, I can't count the number of times I have passed up on opportunities or ducked out from dreams because of fear that I wasn't enough or might fail. Sound familiar? I struggled with being my own friend and advocating for my goals because I thought someone else might be better for the job. Well, I'm happy to say that this is a thing of the past.

How did I do it you might ask? How did I eventually pick myself up, dust myself off and keep going? The first thing I did and still do to this day is rely on one of my favorite underdog stories—all of the *Rocky* films. As corny as it might sound, I love the story of Rocky and his ability to triumph in spite of all types of adversity. We've all seen adversity in our lives, and it helps to have something to hold onto during the tough times. It also reminds me of my childhood and times I spent with my father watching the movies. My father fought the ultimate battle with cancer and although he lost his life to the disease, he showed me what overcoming really means.

In addition, I learned over time that you just need to put one foot in front of the other and keep moving forward. You must keep moving in spite of fear. As Brené Brown says, "You can choose courage or you can choose comfort. But you cannot have both." I don't know about you, but I choose courage.

Believe me, I wasn't always this way. I grew up in a loving but ambitious family that taught me the value of hard work. You throw this on the fire of perfectionism and it can go haywire. Early in life, I held myself to impossibly high standards, had stomach issues as a student and worried that I might not get all straight A's for the 8th semester in a row. I was a habitual gold star chaser that was so worried about being "right" or "perfect" that I often missed the joy and fun in everyday moments. Unfortunately, these feelings of perfectionism and not being good enough followed me into my career and my family life.

At one point in my career, I was in line for a promotion to a sales manager position of an investment department. My feelings of not being adequately prepared or right for the job actually came to pass. My boss at the time told me that I was being passed up for the role because I didn't have prior sales experience. I was angry at my boss for being looked over for the promotion and felt like a victim. What I didn't realize until later is that I was creating this result by believing I couldn't do it! My thoughts were creating my actions which resulted in the outcome of not getting the job.

Unfortunately, this wasn't the only time that this happened to me. I guess I needed a few lessons for the idea that I was enough to really sink in. At another position, I was given a great management opportunity. The role would allow me to expand my skills, manage new areas and truly grow in my field. Instead of taking the bull by the horns with the opportunity, I almost squandered it and got myself fired! After six months, my boss told me that I wasn't the right fit for the role. Again, the reason that I wasn't the right fit is that I never really stepped into it. I didn't fully own the job because I didn't feel capable, so my boss didn't get the opportunity to see what I could truly do.

After these experiences, I knew I needed to change. I knew that I needed to get my head on straight and persevere through my own doubts. I needed to become my own advocate and friend.

Here's how I did it:

1. **I learned who was in my cheering section.**

   Many of us think as a default that our family members or childhood friends are our "tribe", the people that will cheer us on no matter what. Your family and old friends may fit the bill or they may not. And that's OK. I ask you to really, really think about who will stand behind you, no matter how crazy your dream. No matter what you want to do. The person or people that you can call with the wildest idea and they will support you in it. If you have 1–2 people like this in your life, congratulations. Consider yourself lucky. And if you don't, don't worry. Just be you, keep getting out there and being vulnerable and you'll find them eventually. It's a big job to fill after all.

2. **I had an amazing mentor.**

   If you don't have a mentor, get one. Like immediately. Again, a mentor isn't necessarily your boss or your mom. It's the person that will see your light, even before you see it. It's the person that will push you to the point of irritation, but you love them for it so you come back for more. It's the person who gives you the tools and insight to become a better version of yourself. If you take anything from this story, get a mentor. You can do this by seeking one out. Ask someone you respect or admire to mentor you. I bet they'll say yes and you'll be better off for it.

3. **I sought out help when I needed it.**

   After my daughter was born, I experienced postpartum anxiety and depression. I didn't know that I had this at the time, even though I went to all of the baby prep classes. The anxiety and depression really threw my perfectionism into overdrive. I never felt like I was a good mom and that I was doing enough for my daughter. I felt like a failure and couldn't do the job. Does it sound similar to my prior experiences? I eventually realized what was going on and sought out the help I needed. I'm happy to say that I'm now mentally stronger and no longer beat myself up about not being a good mom. I know I'm doing the best I can, and that's good enough for me.

4. I put my oxygen mask on first.

You know when you listen to the safety video on a plane, they tell you to put your oxygen mask on first? Do you really do that? Do you carve out time for yourself? Honestly, this one is still a work in progress for me. I've come to learn that if you put your oxygen mask on first, you'll be a better and happier version of yourself. This will translate to you being a better spouse, girlfriend, mother, sister, friend and employee. It is also positive fuel for feeling good enough in your life. If you set aside time for yourself to read, get a manicure, go to the movies, read a book or have coffee with a friend, you've put your needs first for a few minutes. This is worth it because you're worth it.

5. I understand that my thoughts create my reality.

I'll admit that there have been plenty of times where I felt like a victim in my own life and career. They were times where the weight of the thoughts "I'm not good enough" felt crushing and I didn't feel like doing anything but blame others. I've learned I will get nowhere fast with this attitude. If it's going to be in my life, whether that's a loving relationship with my husband or daughter, a great friendship or a rewarding career, I need to take responsibility for my own happiness and what I think of myself. If I play the old tapes of "I'm not good enough", "Who do you think you are?" or "I can't do this", I will get more of the same in my life. This negative tape will dictate my outcome. I will get more of what I think about. To change your circumstances, you need to change your thinking.

6. I realize this is an ongoing practice.

I thought once I felt good enough that it would be a permanent state of being. I know now that this is not the case. Life happens after all. We all get our confidence shaken or experience fear from time to time. It's how we manage through these times that counts. It's the choices we make in times of adversity, whether to stay safe in fear or choose courage, that define us. And unfortunately this means that this is an ongoing practice. You're going to need to call on your cheering section when you're down. You're going to need to get pushed from your mentor to get to yet another level. You're going to need to seek help or put your oxygen mask on periodically. There will even be times that you forget everything you learn and decide to feel like a victim or that you're not good enough. It's all part of the process. And that's OK.

7. I've watched a little Rocky now and again.

Yes, there are times I put my pajamas on immediately after a tough day at work, grab a blanket and revisit my childhood hero, Rocky. There are times when vegging out or doing something comfortable can help when you're not feeling good enough, when you need to get pumped up to do something or simply need a reminder of how great you really are. I believe that knowing the movies, songs, quotes, books and more that comfort and inspire you can not only tell you more about yourself, but also give you the resources to keep moving forward when things get tough.

After hearing my story, I hope you feel differently about your own. I want nothing more than for you to go after that job, make that new friend, go get that mentor and become friends with yourself. Know that you can do anything in which you put your effort, heart and mind. Life is hard enough as it is, so don't bully yourself with unkind words of not being good enough or setting the bar so high that you can't possibly reach your goals. Perfection is not realistic and is a waste of time.

Learn to be nice to yourself. Being nice to yourself is a pathway to your dreams. Most importantly, choose courage every chance you get. Courage in the morning. Courage in the meeting. Courage with your kids. Courage in a difficult conversation. Just courage.

"When we spend our lives waiting until we're perfect or bulletproof before we walk into the arena, we ultimately sacrifice relationships and opportunities that may not be recoverable, we squander our precious time, and we turn our backs on our gifts, those unique contributions that only we can make. Perfect and bulletproof are seductive, but they don't exist in the human experience." — Brené Brown

Jennifer Pestikas

Jennifer Pestikas was born and raised in the Chicagoland area. She graduated with a French and Spanish degree from Indiana University. During her studies, she lived abroad in France and obtained a political science certificate from the Institut D'Etudes Politiques (IEP). Jennifer also has earned a Masters of Business Administration from Lake Forest Graduate School of Management. She holds her securities and insurance licenses.

After college, Jennifer began her career in the investment services industry. Throughout her years in investments, Jennifer covered a three state territory where she trained investment advisors, wrote marketing plans for over thirty financial institutions and assisted in driving the operational impact for investment programs. Jennifer moved on to manage the sales and operations of a successful wealth management division for a large financial institution.

Jennifer then added to her skill set by taking on the challenge of managing multiple departments, including marketing and human resources. She has been instrumental in the development of brands, social media strategy, new websites and products and services for multiple financial institutions. After being inspired to help others, Jennifer developed an innovative leadership program at her organization. In 2016, Jennifer was honored as a Woman to Watch by the Credit Union Times.

Jennifer has most recently obtained her corporate coaching designation with IPEC and started her own life and leadership coaching business, How Winning is Done. Jennifer is passionate about helping women who experience perfectionism and self-doubt to learn how to become friends with themselves and take purposeful action in their lives and careers.

When Jennifer is not working to make positive change in her organization or helping women be the best version of themselves, she can be found having fun with her husband and daughter. Jennifer can be found at howwinningisdone.com.

Jennifer Pestikas

How Winning is Done

1124 Tamarack Lane

Libertyville, IL 60048

847-207-9405

info@howwinningisdone.com

howwinningisdone.com

Kathy Rosner

Great Things Happen Outside of Your Comfort Zone

"We are born for greatness. Magic happens when you step outside of your comfort zone."

These are wise words from a wise and well respected man that I know named McKay Christensen.

We all strive for a comfortable life. It's human nature to want to be comfortable, and yet, amazing things can happen when you face your fears, accept change, and take that step (or leap) outside of your comfort zone!

I know it has happened to me many times in my life.

Growing up in the Catholic girl's school system, we were groomed to attend college and become nurses, teachers—or nuns. I knew that being a nun was definitely not in my future so I chose teaching and went on to attend NIU. I received my teaching degree and prepared for a secure future.

Unfortunately, after graduation, I discovered there were no teaching positions available. I had to quickly create a Plan B. It involved something that was not what I was being groomed for and completely outside of my comfort zone. I became a flight attendant!

That choice led me to a 32-year airline career with two different major airlines. The first sixteen years were with Eastern and took me through the tumultuous 70's from hot pants to hijackings, airline strikes and a *total shutdown* of the airline during the Gulf War. There was no warning, no paycheck, and no pension.

Many of my flight attendant friends went on to fly with other airlines. They encouraged me to interview with American Airlines. However, I was hesitant to interview. I was the mom of two small boys and the thought of leaving them for six weeks of training was very upsetting. It was one of the most difficult and uncomfortable choices I would ever make. Nevertheless, I didn't really have an alternative. I moved outside of my comfort zone, trained with American and became an American Airlines flight attendant.

I did actually like working with American. That difficult decision later allowed us to travel as a family and provided a lifetime of travel benefits.

As I was "flying along" and enjoying my career something happened that changed the face of commercial flying forever. That something was 9/11. On that day, the world changed and along with it, the entire travel industry. Flying would never be the same.

It was time for a career change but I needed to continue to fly to pay the bills.

During that time, I hired a home organizer named Christine to help me clean out my crawl space. I thought we might have to move, if I was going to leave American Airlines.

While cleaning off the very dusty crawl space area, I brought in some of my household cleaners. Christine gasped. "Don't spray those toxic cleaners in here. Read the back of the bottle. It says to use only in a well-ventilated area, which this crawl space is not. It also says to wear a mask and gloves and not to spray around your animals. It also says that it may cause breathing problems and I have a touch of asthma." She went on to explain that these chemicals were probably why I get so many headaches and why my sons have skin, allergy and breathing issues.

She said the bottom line was that I needed to detox my home. When I realized what I was doing by bringing toxic products into my home purchased from our local grocery store, I thought to myself, "What kind of mother am I?" Christine gave me the name of a woman named Debra who she said could show me how to detox my home with safe, non-toxic "green" cleaners.

Little did I know that when I stepped outside of my crawl space that day, I would be stepping outside my comfort zone again with a career change! Debra shared with me the name of a company called Melaleuca. I anxiously became a customer wanting to get every chemical-laden product out of my house as quickly as possible. Debra was a wonderful mentor. The more she shared her knowledge about safer products, the more I knew I had to share this information with my friends and family and anyone else I cared about. She also saw my potential as a leader. I soon began building a business with this relatively unknown company with an unusual name.

Everything about my Melaleuca journey just felt right from the start. As a flight attendant I was always sharing with others great restaurants, where to shop for sales, jewelry and crafts made by friends or other attendants, and more. Therefore, sharing a safer way to shop was an easy and natural thing for me to do.

My family members then started having amazing experiences. My headaches disappeared; my son's skin rashes and allergies disappeared. Colds and flus disappeared as our immune systems were no longer compromised by toxins in our home. How could I *not* share this with others I cared about?

Once we packed up every chemical laden cleaner and personal care product in our home—everything that touched our skin or we would breathe in the air, we took that box out to the curb on garbage pickup day. Much to our surprise, the trash man knocked on our door and informed us that he couldn't put some of the products in his truck as they had the potential to cause chemical combustion. He showed me where it indicated on the label that special disposal methods were needed since they were "hazardous materials." I was once again in shock that these were the same products I was spraying around my house thinking I was doing something good for my family!! The trash man gave me a "hazmat" sticker and said I needed to take all of the cleaning products that contained bleach and ammonia to a special facility to dispose of them! I thanked him and decided to leave the products by the curb until the next morning when I could drive them to the Hazmat center.

Imagine my surprise when I went out the next day and someone had taken the box of toxic cleaners! I then decided that if the trash pickup company would not take those cleaners, no one should be using them in their homes. It became my mission to educate everyone I knew about what I had learned and to offer people the benefits of a non-toxic home. Word of mouth is powerful.

I soon learned that "going green" was already growing in popularity. There was huge receptivity especially from mother's when they saw the research I shared on how household chemicals were the main culprits in the rising rates of asthma, allergies, eczema and even learning disabilities and behavioral problems! I almost felt guilty as my monthly referral check for showing others how to shop with Melaleuca went from the hundreds to the thousand. Much of it was residual and would arrive whether or not I shared Melaleuca with anyone that month.

One day I really discovered the value of this chance encounter with the world of non-toxic products and the residual income it created.

I was hit with the news that I needed to have surgery that would prevent me from flying for at least a few months. I had no more airline sick time left so the only way I would get a check from the airline was if I could fly which was impossible. However, my Melaleuca check kept showing up month after month—and even grew because people with whom I'd shared the products were sharing them with others!! This business was not all about me and what I was doing day to day. *It was then that I realized the power of residual income!*

This experience appeared to be the eye opener that I needed to jump in with both feet. It motivated me to move out of my comfort zone once again and to make a complete career change. As I weighed the pros and cons, there were flight attendants who thought I was crazy to give up flying to "sell soap"! I also questioned whether this was the right thing to do. However, my intuition told me that this is what I needed. I faced the fear of leaving the only career I had ever known, to build my Melaleuca business full-time from home.

Sixteen years after having made that decision, I have now come full circle. I am back to the career that I was groomed for in Catholic school and for which I obtained my college degree. I now educate others on how to have wellness on a budget and build a solid residual income from home. Melaleuca is a noble business. I enjoy helping moms earn significant income from home, so they can be there when their kids need them the most. I enjoy helping others pay off debt, plan for retirement or buy a car or their dream home. It's the peace of mind in having choices of my own and giving others a business that provides them with the freedom of choice that keeps me engaged in Melaleuca. It's all about helping others and making a difference for our planet at the same time.

So how does DPWN (Dynamic Professional Women's Network) fit into all this?

In 2010, a neighbor kept inviting me to a local chapter meeting. I told her I was too busy with my business and didn't have time for a women's networking group. She was persistent, so I finally said that I would go with her to the next meeting. However, the category of Health and Wellness was already taken at that chapter. A few days later, Christie Ruffino, the Founder and President of DPWN called and asked if I would like to start a new Chapter in the Barrington area. Start a new chapter? Talk about stepping outside my comfort zone! I knew nothing about network groups or DPWN, but since it wasn't the first time I'd decided to step outside my comfort zone. I agreed to take on the challenge of Chapter Director.

I'd built a successful Melaleuca team of leaders, so thought I could handle this. However, now I was dealing with women from different businesses with different agendas –all wanting more business for themselves. It wasn't working as planned and I was ready to step away. That was when a few of our founding Barrington chapter members got together and decided that whatever it took, we were going make it work. We decided to build our chapter around supporting and helping others. We always asked ourselves how we could help each member grow. Our mission statement became: "Empowering women to be their very best." As soon as we adopted that mission statement, our Barrington Chapter began to grow.

"I've always believed that one woman's success can only help another woman's success." —Gloria Vanderbilt

The past seven years have been a wonderful learning experience. I learned that different women are passionate about different things in different ways. We all want success. We all want to be living with purpose. We all want validation—and we all want to make a difference.

We all learned to respect our differences and realized we can learn from each other.

We have had up to 28 influential members at the peak of our chapter growth.

The Dynamic Professional Women's Network itself has a powerful mission statement:

"We are a dedicated group of success-orientated business professionals setting goals to increase our business and develop personally. We help each other's businesses grow with valuable referrals and assist each other by providing counsel in our particular areas of expertise."

We continue to learn from each other, as new members come and seasoned members move on.

There is no more effective tool for personal growth than the empowerment of women. Each member brings a special gift of her knowledge to share. We will continue to learn from each other as our members come and go.

I am now stepping outside of my comfort zone again by agreeing to write and become one of the authors for Volume 5 "Resilient Women" in the

Overcoming Mediocrity series.

Christie has asked me to write my story for the previous four books, but I wasn't ready. "I'm not an author. What knowledge could I possibly share?" I would tell her. To which she would reply, "We all have a story to share!"

I do believe that we are all more influential than we may think. Our children, families, co-workers and friends are all watching what we do and how we live. What do you want your legacy to be? What do you want to be most remembered for in your lifetime? Probably not for simply living a comfortable life. How about for facing your fears and making change happen? This takes courage, but it is worth it. I do believe that ordinary people can do extra ordinary things!

I'd like to share with you 9 tips to keep in mind once you've made the decision to change your life and change your future:

1. Let go of the past. You have a spotless future.

2. Trust your intuition. You know in your gut what's best for you.

3. Do not let the opinions of others define who you are.

4. Accept your past mistakes as opportunities for growth.

5. Let go of people that disrespect or use you.

6. Embrace people who believe in you.

7. Stop doubting yourself!

8. Trust that everything does happen for a reason.

9. Accept fully that you are on the path meant for you.

Discover the beat of your own heart. Be that influential woman that can make a difference in the lives of others.

"Be the change you wish to see in the world." —Mahatma Gandhi

I say be the change you want your life to be...or the change you want your business to be.

In our ever-changing world, now more than ever, we must learn to adapt, accept, and embrace more change; so put fear aside. Step outside your comfort zone and watch as great things begin to happen in your life!

Kathy Rosner

Kathy's life and career choices have taken the course of three cycles of change, each over a 16 year cycle. She graduated with a teaching degree from NIU, but was unable to find a teaching position. She, therefore, decided to get adventurous and become a flight attendant for the next 32 years (including 16 with Eastern Airlines and 16 with American Airlines). After 9/11, the world changed and so did Kathy. She decided to retire from the airline industry and work from home. She can now be home for her sons and family when they need her. "Going Green" was becoming popular after 9/11, so she decided it was time for a career change. Kathy became a marketing executive for Melaleuca. com. She was very fortunate to be able to work from her home. She loves educating families on how to keep their homes healthy and safe—wellness on a budget. She started www.CEOmoms.biz and now teaches other Moms how they can work their own business from home and be there when their kids need them most! The 3–16 year career cycles have now come full circle, back to where she started with a teaching degree. Kathy will continue this career of helping others with Melaleuca.com for many years past 16!

Kathy has been the DPWN Barrington Chapter Director since it began in 2010. Many women have started and grown their own businesses through DPWN Barrington membership.

Kathy Rosner
Melaleuca.com
2251 Inverray Rd
Inverness, IL 60067
847-991-4242
kathyarosner@gmail.com
www.BusinessThatMakesSense.com

Michelle L. Sutter

Recalculating: Life's GPS

As I reflect back on my 48 years, I realize that for a long time, my life's journey had been strikingly similar to that of a GPS. It was recalculating my route, even when not asked. I was extremely diligent in charting my course, making lists, setting goals and doing everything I could to be on time, in time and making the most of my time. However, when I least expected it, life's GPS sent me down a terrifying road, filled with a myriad of potholes. It was a trip filled with personal heartache and discovery. Whether in your car, or in life, these directional changes, or *recalculating* as my friendly British GPS lady loves to say far too often, can provide the most unexpected life lessons.

In 2012, my Life GPS went on a life changing journey. In an instant, I went from cruising along on top of the world...to being lost and ultimately crashing into a "ditch" along life's road! With hands clenched to my steering wheel of life, I looked up only to see a billboard with flashing lights that read, "MICHELLE, YOU HAVE A RARE GENETIC DISEASE!" and, "PS. THERE IS NO CURE!"

Prior to the diagnosis, my days were filled with two years of symptoms, wrong turns and misdiagnoses. Often hearing from medical professionals that it was stress, anxiety, or most frustrating, only in my head. Unfortunately, it was the reality for many with unexplained, or hard to diagnose symptoms. The first real discovery came with a diagnosis of severe anemia. Since traveling down a road so long with no answers, I quickly became excited just to have one: *Anemia. Hmmm? I learned that anemia was a symptom and not a condition.* The following 60 days involved numerous blood tests, doctor appointments, MRIs, CT scans and x-rays. If there was a test to take, I took it. From lupus to Lyme to XYZ disease. Yet, all they could offer as a solution was a hysterectomy, since it was the likely the culprit of the anemia. Or, so they thought.

Sadly I knew my other symptoms were different. I lay in bed late at night wondering… *What was I missing? What had we not tested for?* The last test in the long line scheduled was a colonoscopy. The doctors hesitated, because at the time I was only 42, eight years shy of the recommended screening guidelines. Refusing to leave any stone unturned, I had to emphatically insist on the colonoscopy. I knew it was important, because two years earlier my dad had a portion of his colon removed due to excessive polyps, and his surgeon advised all of his children to be mindful and to get checked regularly. In hindsight, I am glad that I listened. (Interesting enough his surgeon never mentioned a genetic connection, or disease…just to take note.)

The doctors finally agreed and exam day arrived, with the full fanfare of what it takes to prep for this lovely procedure. (I'll just say it's a very cleansing experience.) Telling myself, *you've got this Michelle, remember you are only 42.*

As they wheeled me to recovery, in my sedated state, I heard the doctor tell my husband that I had more polyps in my colon than he had seen the entire week of all patients combined. There were far too many to remove, and too far advanced to attempt removing individually. He advised us to immediately schedule an appointment with the Emory Genetic Cancer Center in Atlanta. He strongly believed that I had a rare genetic condition he had never seen in person but had only studied in medical school twenty years ago. Kudos to my doc for his keen sense of recall.

This definitely wasn't planned — where was this new road taking me?

The hardest appointments of all during this time were with my genetic counselor. I sat numb, in shock when the test results were read, revealing that I did indeed have this mysterious rare disease, in clinical terms a genetic mutation (alteration) of the APC gene. I sat in a fog, as they advised me that immediate surgery was needed, there was a 98% chance of colon cancer within three years or sooner. It was not as simple as surgery to remove the damaged organ, that didn't mean I was cured, the growths (polyps) often move to other organs, once the colon is removed. The pamphlet that was provided outlined the eight other cancers associated with this gene mutation with predictors of when they would hit in my now likely shortened lifetime. It included everything from brain tumors to colon cancer and, all organs in between. I don't care how half-glass full I thought I was, this was tough news to hear.

The double-whammy was that my children had a 50/50 percent chance of having the disease as well. Hence the word, *familial*...how could this be? I wanted to scream at the top of my lungs, "Throw all you've got at me, but leave my kids alone!" Sadly, no matter how loud you yell, Life's GPS calmly continues to simply give direction to move on.

A few weeks after my diagnosis, the phone call came with the results of my children's genetic tests. I held my breath, and said a prayer before answering. There was no small talk. I just needed to know. It wasn't the news I wanted to hear. I sobbed so I hard I couldn't even say goodbye. My son had escaped it but sadly my daughter did not. I was crushed. Her diagnosis was harder to accept than even my own. Words of "not fair," "why God?" came to mind along with unbearable guilt. We told my son first. He was elated. Then, with tears in my eyes, I turned to my daughter, her hands in mine, to deliver the news that no mother should have to, that she tested positive for the disease. Her first words to me were, "Am I going to die?" I couldn't answer her. It took everything I had in me to keep my composure, not wanting her to know how broken I was inside. That day, right there and then, at our dining room table, this cause took on a whole new meaning to our mother/daughter life trip.

In a nutshell, we lack the chromosome that suppresses tumor growth. The key to our survival is to be diligent with our biopsies every year from "bow to stern", removing any new growths as they occur. Each year when we visit the Cleveland Clinic, I ask myself, "Is this the year?"

I didn't have time to be sick and rare disease was certainly not on my *To-Do List*. I couldn't turn around, or ask for an alternate route. I had no choice but to forge on and find my way.

In the weeks following my diagnosis, WebMD and Google became my new best friend late into the night researching everything I could. My results? There were more ominous posts of doom and gloom for a disease that most people have never heard of. My surgeon told me on my first visit that surgery was my only option. He said that I should feel blessed, since most people don't live as long as I had up to that point. If I had waited for a colonoscopy at the typical age of 50, it likely would have proven to be deadly.

This year marks my five year "diagnosis anniversary". It has been a roller coaster ride with good days and bad days, cancer scares, hospital stays, dehydration, and blockages, which are all by-products of my condition. My daughter is an amazing young woman. Starting annual colonoscopies at sixteen is just not fun. Her spirit is positive and I am so very blessed to have her by my side.

I tell my story not to gain sympathy, but to gain awareness, and most importantly, to remind myself and others to enjoy the view on the road of life, even if the road is not chosen. With this diagnosis, I often wonder how many years I have left in this journey called "Life." Only God knows. All I know is to work daily to appreciate and make the most of every minute, hour, and day I have. Since being diagnosed, I have only met two other individuals, in-person, who have this disease aside from my daughter and me, which is hard. The first few I was blessed to have connected with via social groups have since passed. One special lady I will always hold dear in my heart was, Danielle, from England. Danielle and I were the same age when we were diagnosed and both of us had two children. For her, the diagnosis was too late. The cancer had spread beyond the doctor's control. She died in 2014, leaving behind her loving family. Just last year, she would have become a grandmother. Our hours of chat helped me in the early days—to have someone who understood what we were going through and who had been there. Her death was a hard blow and an awful reminder that my days are also numbered. My team of doctors told me that if I stick with them, they will help get me to my seventies. However, I am determined to make it to the ripe old age of 90!

During my entire life, I have been a list maker. A day doesn't go by that I don't have my notebook by my side. For years I have been asked, "How do you get so much done in your day?" My answer…"My lists."

Since my diagnosis, my "to-do lists" have become life's roadmap. My grocery lists and daily to-dos are now more about my bucket list, my future, and my children's future as shown below. Though my destination is not clear, my journey will be mapped by me.

What can I do with the gifts that God has given to me?

1. Champion the cause relative to hereditary colon cancer and rare diseases.

2. Make lasting memories and traditions for my children to treasure and carry on.

3. Appreciate daily the power of family as a loving wife, mother and step-mother.

4. Be a role model, mentor, and coach to those looking to achieve their next level.

5. Be charitable, giving of my time, and resources to others less fortunate than I.

6. Be adventurous, and break out of my comfort zone!

As crazy as it appears, the planner in me has clearly outlined my departing wishes to my sweet husband (in list format, of course). He rolled his eyes and said, "Why? Isn't this a little morbid?" "Not at all," I replied. I want my funeral to be a call to action to those in attendance, not a weepy, sad event. My life, though it may be shorter than originally planned, has been blessed. I want others to appreciate the importance of the road they are on in life and to make the most of every day. *Cue the list...*

- Do a kind act for someone you know or, don't even know; pay it forward

- Pay for that person's drink behind you at Starbucks. It might just make his/her day.

- Send a card to a friend "just because," not because Hallmark told you to.

- Text someone you lost contact with and let them know you are thinking of them.

- Say "please," "thank-you" and "you're welcome."

- Give hugs; 12 second hugs *(sounds nutty—but, try it)*.

- Be true to your word

- Make an impactful difference in the world around you...support a cause financially or by volunteering. The list of causes is plenty. From Red Nose Day to Wear Red Day—have fun with it! It's all about advocacy and awareness.

When I write it down, I see how it easy it is! Most importantly, I want others to take care of themselves. Get your mammogram; schedule that colonoscopy you've been putting off, if something seems amiss, don't ignore it. Preventive care is named that for a reason—early detection can saves lives. If my sixteen year old daughter can do it, you can too!

Next time life's GPS sends you astray, and starts recalculating unexpectedly, may I suggest you grab a pen, make a list and get to work on making this world a better place. As a dear friend once told me—WRITE IT DOWN. MAKE IT HAPPEN!

Whatever happens, take a deep breath, hold on tight and get ready for the ride; I am here to say it will be okay!

This story is dedicated to my daughter Lyndsey Elaine Sutter

Rare diseases affect 1 in 10 Americans, 30 million people in the United States, and 350 million people globally. Over 7,000 distinct rare diseases exist and approximately 80 percent are caused by faulty genes. The National Institutes of Health estimates that 50% of people affected by rare diseases are children, making rare diseases one of the most deadly and debilitating for children worldwide. To learn more visit www.globalgenes.org

World Rare Disease Day (*February 28th each year*)

Colon Cancer Awareness Month is held annually in March (*Wear Blue*)

Michelle L. Sutter

Michelle was raised in western New York, braving the snow and cold for the first 30 years of her life, before settling in Atlanta, GA with her husband, Rick and children, Lyndsey and Christopher. She currently serves as the Sr. Vice President of Employee Benefit Consulting. With her background in healthcare consulting, she uses this platform to educate her clients and their employees and anyone she meets, on how to best navigate today's healthcare system. Michelle shares her personal health story as a way to forge a personal connection and to emphasize the importance of preventive care, wellness and consumer advocacy. Since her diagnosis in 2012 of a rare disease, Michelle has worked to champion the cause that relates to Hereditary Cancers and Rare Diseases.

You can connect with Michelle via email at: SutterMum@gmail.com or, follow "SutterMum" on Facebook & Instagram. If you are looking to network in the Atlanta market, Michelle invites you to join the Gwinnett Women's Small Business Collective (GWSBC) that she serves as moderator for via www.MeetUp.com

Fun Fact about Michelle: she collects Santa's, with currently over 350 in her collection, and most years has between 9 to 13 fully decorated trees in her home. Perhaps being born on St. Nicholas Day had an impact!

Michelle L. Sutter
Suwanee, GA
SutterMum@gmail.com

Sherry E.T. Rauch-Dehbozorgi

Never Take a NO from Someone Who Was Never Empowered to Give You a YES in the First Place

"Never take a no from someone who was never empowered to give you a yes in the first place." —SEDT

It means NEVER GIVE UP, not on your business, not on your loved ones and not even on yourself. It also includes what people speak over you, say about you or even say to your face. I made up this quote because I was tired of people telling me "NO", that I was not good enough or I have power over you to stop you in your tracks. All of my life, I was hearing that and/or attracting the energy into my life. I found that either of two things would happen. It would upset me enough and light a fire underneath me or it would tear me down to the core and take the wind out of my sails. From a very early age, I heard and felt that I was never good enough, a loser or too dumb to educate (my father's words). I would hear that at home, at school and everywhere I went. However, it was mostly in my own head. It rang like a bell for years, leading to depression and suicide attempts over a 30-year period.

I have always known that I was different. I never seemed to fit into society. I was brutally bullied, from the first through the twelfth grades, because of undiagnosed learning disabilities (dyslexia, ADD and autism). I was put into the lower level classes and fell through the cracks in the educational system. This fueled my anger and depression over the years. I got jobs that allowed me to be alone (paper routes, entrepreneurship). I did not do team sports, but instead I preferred martial arts, kickboxing and ring fighting, in order to cope with my lack of socialization skills and anger issues.

Those feelings persisted through a violently abusive, failed marriage. It is never good when two broken people get together and not know how broken they actually are. He unfortunately turned to alcohol to drown his pain. I could not afford to give into addictions. I had to be the responsible parent. They needed me to be a rock, and I could not afford to let my family down while he needed to figure out things in his own life. However, I took that job seriously by putting their needs over mine and sacrificing a lot for them. I also found out that it was a generational curse in my family, for the woman to attract abusive broken alcoholic men. I made sure that it stopped with me, so my children would rise above those painful life lessons. Through all of the emotional pain that they had to endure, we all did our best to survive each day while dealing with our own internal emotional issues. When I saw the first signs that my children inherited my learning issues, I made sure they got the help they needed to be successful. I used every resource to fulfill my kid's needs, leaning heavily on the school social workers for parenting advice and support.

I can tell you that healing did come. After thousands of tear-filled nights and many of days with knots in my stomach, I started to attract good life lessons. However, it was a decision to trust and focus on the positive aspects in my life and expand those moments and feelings instead of focusing on all the negative, which surrounded me. I knew that I was placed on this Earth to make a huge impact, one life at a time, if necessary. This did not happen overnight. It was a long road. Many friends and loved ones saw me through "the crazy times". However, as I listened to positive books, hours of YouTube and uplifting speakers, things started to change. I learned to love myself bit by bit. Some days were good and some days were not. However, when I found myself getting caught up in the mortal realm of life, I would start to hate myself again. I, therefore, had to learn to focus on my higher self. When I did, I found miracles happening because the power of love and connecting to the universal one mind. I found my life's purpose, which is to be a life toucher and to pour Divine blessings and wisdom into others. Always remember that you deserve all the blessings that the universe is giving. You should know they are for you. You must accept them with open arms and share them through you. If the blessings are meant to be in your life, they will be.

Enough of my Herstory, let's get back to this quote. The quote is: "Never take a no from someone who was never empowered to give you a yes in the first place" It helped me in sales. I have always had a natural talent in the area of sales and marketing. I just get it on many levels. I have had this gift since the age of five, selling Girl Scout cookies for my sister. My pitch was… "YOU need some cookies" with a big smile. I was only five. Who could resist a positive little girl? In sales, you will get 100 NO's before you get that one YES! You will also get discouraged, because after a while, it will feel personal. However, that only means that you will have to either sharpen your skills, ask more people or find the right product that fills many people's pain points. By not stopping after the first no that you hear from someone, it helps build a thicker skin or a deeper relationship with that person. This is because you are adding value and a service into their lives. Since I was the baby of the family, I hated to be told "NO". I always asked WHY NOT? Why can't you fulfill my wishes or my requests? Don't you love me? (Yes, I equated it with self-love too). I would rarely take no for an answer. Therefore, I would keep asking or debating it until I got a YES! My children inherited that trait from me. That is one thing I love most about them. I know that they will not settle for injustice or mediocrity in their lives. With that skill, there has been many spirited debates in this house over the years!

By not settling for a NO, you are not letting others put limitations upon your soul. Find another way to get that YES. When it comes, know that you deserve that blessing. It is for you and someone said yes to your desires. Celebrate it and live in that moment. You should make it a great life memory. This also works when you are blocked by customer service reps in a large company. They are never given the power to say yes, or to truly handle your issue. My advice is to go up the chain of command. If you can get your ideas heard by the CEO of that company, they have more power to say YES. However, make sure that your idea makes sense for them and fills a need within their company. It shouldn't be just your need for a sales quota. You must service your customers' needs or be of service to them. You will find it easier to get that yes that you are looking for when you put yourself in their shoes, and learn what their pain points are. We are all connected in this universe. When others can feel your heart, you won't have to hear a NO. That is because they will be empowered to give you a yes in the first place.

All those wonderful blessings that others were pouring into me to help me heal, gave me the desire to help raise others up. I created SEDT Business Development with a strong desire to be the catalyst to help others get to the next phase of their evolution, by sharing what knowledge was downloaded into me. I naturally gravitated toward social media. It was a way for me to reach a huge audience, without needing to leave the comfort or security of my own home. It was ideal for me, because I needed to be there full time for my children. It gave me a voice and a platform to the outside world. When I could not go to a networking group, I searched out the leaders or the movers and shakers and built relationships with them online. I took those skills and built a large network. I now teach others what I know about growing your business through online means. I look forward to helping you grow your business one day soon.

In conclusion, my advice is that when you are feeling like the world keeps telling you NO, I want you to do is dig down deep inside of you and find that little YES. Put it on a card and hold onto that spark of dreams from the divine spirit. Focus on that, give love and light to it, and build on that dream daily. The universe will bring you water, dirt and sunlight for it to grow. Just keep saying yes to that dream in your heart. I am so grateful for all of the people who sewed blessings or life lessons into me, so I could share my story and my heart with you today. I pray that my life story gave you hope and inspiration to keep going and never give up. When it comes your time to shine, no one can possibly stand in your way of your Divine Spirit. So, rise up and live your joy to show the world your light.

Blessings of love and light, Sherry ET Rauch/Dehbozorgi

Sherry E.T. Rauch/Dehbozorgi

Sherry Rauch/Dehbozorgi started SEDT Business Development in 2011, because she saw a need to help small business owner market themselves and their businesses on social media. She now partners with several businesses in the greater Chicagoland area. She specializes in targeted lead generation that drives traffic from your social media to your website, optimizing your social media profiles for maximum impact and generating effective social campaigns to blast your message to targeted social media groups. It involves cross marketing your message on several platforms to spread the word of your company or event to a larger audience. To condense the learning curve, Sherry offers training seminars to teach small business owners, MLM'ers, real estate and insurance agents, techniques to sharpen and advance their marketing skills on social media. She offers both a 45 and 90-day social media program with one on one coaching, mastermind sessions, and weekly page management all intended to help you gain likes, contacts and be able to pull quality leads from your social media platforms. Sherry looks forward to working with you to make your business grow. She can be messaged on these social media platforms Facebook, LinkedIn, Instagram, YouTube and Rally Point. If you like more conventional methods, she can be reached either via my website SEDTBIZ. com, email SEDTBIZ100@gmail.com, and via phone 815-931-9386.

Sherry E.T. Rauch/Dehbozorgi
SEDT Business Development
21752 Ives Ct.
Plainfield, IL 60544
815-931-9386
sedtbiz100@gmail.com
SEDTbiz.com

Jennifer Truesdale

Brittle, Not Broken

I was twelve years old. I was at my favorite place in the whole world, the Roller Palace. Like we did every Saturday afternoon skate session, we were doing the Hokey Pokey. This time however, I did something I didn't usually do, I fell "putting my whole self in". When I got up off of the floor, I knew something was wrong with my arm. Therefore, I skated over to the guard and calmly said, "Excuse me, I think I just broke my arm." At first they laughed me off, confused by my nonchalance.

The doctor confirmed my thirteenth broken bone, in my right wrist. After reviewing my lengthy history of supposed clumsiness, he turned and asked me to look up. When I met his gaze, he noticed what should be the white part of my eye was instead a deep blue. This is when the doctor changed my life in an instant. This is when I was diagnosed with *Osteogenesis Imperfecta* (OI), or in layman's terms, brittle bone disease.

Over the years I found breaking bones was simply a part of life. It was like the occasional hangnail or getting an oil change. I'd even started setting broken fingers and toes myself, to avoid the wasted day sitting in my local emergency room.

By the time I reached the ripe old age of thirty-eight, I was raising three daughters on Social Security Disability payments. The miniscule monthly benefit only covered a fraction of my mortgage payment, let alone necessities like groceries or utilities.

I was depressed. I was broken. I was broke.

I let the world tell me who I was and how I should act. I let people convince me that with more than sixty breaks, and almost a dozen knee surgeries under my belt, it was time to give up. I was told repeatedly there wasn't anything anyone could do to "fix" me. I was Humpty Dumpty. None of the King's orthopedics, pain clinics, physiatrists, neurologists, knee specialists, physical therapists, chiropractors, acupuncturists, or even shaman were able to put me back together again. My only option was to apply for disability and live off of government assistance for the rest of my life. Believing this, I desperately began the application process.

I spent three years convincing the government they should give me money every month because I was useless. I couldn't cook, clean, or even do laundry myself anymore. I no longer had any value in the job market. In the process of convincing the Social Security Administration, I convinced myself that I was useless as well.

In January 2016, my favorite uncle, who lived clear across the country, was dying. Therefore, I did what any broke niece would do. I used that month's mortgage money to buy plane tickets for my daughter and me to visit him one last time.

During that visit, we got to spend some wonderful last moments with my uncle. However, we couldn't go further than the length of his oxygen tube, which was about 30 feet at most from the oxygen tank. Uncle Bob wanted to go to the beach and have lunch at his favorite Fish and Chips stand. He really wanted to be able to take Katie-Rose, his great-niece, and show her the Santa Monica Pier, a spot we would frequent together whenever I would visit him as a child.

In those days, he was always so excited. We'd jump in the waves, ride the roller coaster, and eat more fried dough than our stomachs could handle. He was constantly wise-cracking, smiling, cracking jokes, and oh boy did he tease me.

With portable oxygen tank in hand, we headed towards the boardwalk and the beach. A few steps later, he was gasping for air and we had to pack up and end our adventure. There would be no wise-cracking or fried dough for us on that last trip together to Santa Monica.

While he was resting in his room, I sat outside by the pool and was reflecting on our day. I came to the realization that my monthly Social Security check was a lot like my uncle's oxygen tube. The disability check kept me tethered, and prevented me from going anywhere. Some quick math revealed that if I didn't make a major change, I would spend the rest of my life trying to live off of $500 a month.

That was the moment when I decided I needed to be done being "disabled". I decided that I would get to rewrite the story and change the outcome for myself and my daughters. I wasn't going to let the world tell me who I was, I would get to decide who I was. If inertia had her way, we would have been hungry, uninsured, and eventually homeless.

I was ready to write a new narrative, in which I was not disabled. I would be a successful business owner. I would be world traveler. I would be a provider for my kids, so that they would have financial stability, and graduate from college debt free.

It was as simple as that. I had let the world tell me who I was for way too long. I had heard so many times that I was "broken," "disabled," and "lucky to be getting Social Security," that I actually believed that bull shit. I believed I was "lucky" to be a single mother of three, living off a fixed income that was one quarter of my mortgage payment. How messed up was that?

When I got home from California, a few days later I went back to work full time. Of course, I still had the all the pains from my injuries, but I no longer let them stop me. I had to stop feeling sorry for myself. I had to stop focusing on all the things I could not do, and instead focus on building up my stamina to be able to do things for myself again. I met with my doctors and came up with a better pain plan. I started taking better care of my body by integrating holistic therapies, like chiropractic and massage, and stopped letting the price prevent me from taking better care of myself.

I remembered years ago, I was told if you truly desire something, with all of your heart and soul, you need to visualize it, believe it and act as if it is true until it actually becomes true. I desired to be an able bodied working woman who could take care of her own children. Therefore, I had to push the pain out of my mind. I had to work hard and I had to put 100% effort into being a healthy woman.

I went back to selling insurance, because it was all that I knew how to do. I took a contract with a new company. I began knocking on 40-50 doors a day trying to make sales. I took many of the company's old, inactive accounts and got people to buy new policies. I drove 900 miles each week going to the out of the way accounts that no one else wanted to service. I was hungry for business. I was willing to do whatever it took. I hired a business coach and with each and every sale, I started to feel better. With each family I helped, I got stronger.

I stopped worrying about what other people thought of me and I let my personality shine. I dyed my hair hot pink, just because I wanted to. I was forty years old with hot pink hair, and I rocked it!

I sold over $222,000 worth of new policies in eleven months. I went from Social Security to a six figure income in just under a year.

No one calls me disabled anymore.

Jennifer Truesdale

Jennifer Truesdale grew up on the North Shore of Massachusetts, spending summers at "Happy Hampton Beach" in New Hampshire, where she was taught the value of hard work at young age, helping her grandparents with their beach motel.

At the age of 12 and after 13 or more broken bones, she was diagnosed with Osteogenesis Imperfecta, (brittle bone disease).

After graduating from school, she had to leave her sweetheart behind to go off to college. She attended the University of Miami, where she landed exactly 10 days before Hurricane Andrew, which was at that time the most destructive hurricane in United States history. Surviving her first hurricane was a life changer. Due to some prior knee injuries, life on campus became too difficult after Andrew ripped it apart. Therefore, Jennifer moved back home.

The only problem was that "home" moved 2,000 miles south.

At home, before she could even put down her suitcase, her mother laid out her life options as she saw them. With a whole four hours to ponder the options, she choose insurance school. She realized she had found a career that she was excited about. However, living 2,000 miles away from her sweetheart was not so exciting, so she packed up and headed north.

Over the years, she had worked in many aspects of the insurance industry, and by the age of forty she found herself a single mom for the second time. Scraping by on Social Security Disability and clipping coupons was not the life she wanted for her children.

After a car accident left her with a traumatic brain injury and a couple of broken bones, she realized that she just couldn't live that way. She went back to work selling insurance and has become a top producer on her Aflac team. She is mentoring new agents and helping change lives.

She has also helped her daughter found the not for profit organization, Solar for Our superheroes, which provides solar panels for real world heroes.

Jennifer Truesdale

True Insurance and Notary Services, Inc.

12 Cogger Street

Hampton, NH 03842

603-929-9070

jenntruesdale@aol.com

jentruesdale.com

Jeanmarie Dwyer-Wrigley

Unlikely Angel

Maybe it was her bright blue eyes, or her easy manner which caused my intuition to go into overdrive the first time I met Nancy. I just knew she was a tell-like-it-is, down to earth, honest kind of woman. Five minutes into our conversation, I made a decision. We would be friends!

She taught a Sunday school class which my son attended. Every Sunday, we would talk and I always suggested that we meet for coffee or lunch during the week.

She told me that with taking care of three daughters, working a part time job and involvement with church activities, her life was a little hectic.

I was disappointed, yet I understood her busyness, for in 1974 we were young mothers, juggling schedules to meet family needs. It appeared that our paths would cross only on Sunday mornings.

One Saturday morning, I attended a church committee fund raising meeting and was surprised to find Nancy at the meeting.

"Are you going to work on the committee?" I asked.

"I don't know. I'm thinking about it."

"Well, it would be great to work with you."

Without replying, she nodded her head.

Four months later, after a committee meeting, Nancy suggested that we go to lunch. It was during lunch that she told me the truth of why we never got together. From the first minute we met, she didn't like me.

"What? You're kidding. I don't understand. Why didn't you like me?"

"I thought you were a fluff brain."

"A fluff brain! What? You thought I was stupid?'

"No, just shallow."

"Well, thank you very much. And how did you come to that conclusion?"

"It was the way you dressed. Always wearing big hats, short skirts and those come hither shoes."

"What are you talking about? That's a horrible thing to say."

"Those open toe, strap around the ankle, high heel shoes. I call them, come hither shoes. Gives the message, woman on the prowl."

I took a deep breath, "I didn't wear those shoes because I was on the prowl. I wore them because I loved them. I admit, I did wear them a lot."

"I noticed."

"Then the heel broke on the left shoe. Haven't found a pair like them since."

"Must be tough."

"Now, let me get this straight. You wouldn't have lunch with me because you thought I was shallow, and a fluff brain. You based this judgment on what I wore?"

"I was wrong. Working with you on the committee made me realize you have a brain. In fact, you are very intelligent."

I felt energy racing though my body. I knew what this meant. I was getting ready to have a temper.

My jaw hurt, so I slowly said, "Well that's big of you to find my brain. You must have looked long and hard to discover it." I tightened my lips and glared at her.

She stared at me. Then her lips began to quiver and suddenly she burst out in a roar of laughter.

I watched her as she swayed in her chair, doubled over the table, clutched her stomach and tried to talk.

Before I knew it, I was laughing with her. That is how we began our friendship.

From the beginning, we were supportive of one another. Nancy encouraged and supported my endeavors. Her support was like a jolt of positive energy and kept me moving through the tough times and having fun during the good ones. Her support was also like a rock, anchoring me to realty and yet allowing me to dream

She was the ra ra "you can do it" type of cheerleader. I admit I took it all, loving it.

In 1979, I was trying to start a women's support group. Despite advertising, appearing on a cable television show, giving lectures and basically pounding the pavement, no one came to the Tuesday Night Women's Support Group.

Oh, women called, said they were interested and even promised to be there. But week after week, on Tuesday night I sat in an empty office.

Despondent, I told Nancy I was going to try it for one more Tuesday. If no one came, then I would give it up and look for work in a mental health facility.

On that Tuesday, I heard footsteps. It was Nancy.

Plopping into a chair, she said, "I just had one horrible day. I need to talk."

The two of us talked for an hour.

As we were leaving she asked "You gonna be here next week?"

"No, well, maybe, yes, I don't know."

"I'm going to stop by next week. If I see the light on, I'll know you are in your office and maybe we'll have coffee or something."

As it turned out, I was in my office and Nancy did come but she didn't come alone. She brought a friend.

"I told Marcy she needs a support group and this is the group to be in."

The three of were together for two hours.

For a couple of weeks, it was just the three of us. Then Marcy brought a friend, who in turn recommended the group to a neighbor.

When there were six women, Nancy left the group.

I learned a valuable lesson about support from Nancy at this time. The "you can do it" message of support turned into an "I believe in you" message. When Nancy came to my office to talk about her rotten day and when she brought a friend to the group, she was showing her belief in me and my abilities by her behavior.

The "I believe in you" message is not a high energy cheerleader type of support. It is a quiet type of energy which soothes self-esteem and charms the soul. It always works in conjunction with the giver's behavior.

Who would have thought that on that Saturday afternoon in 1974, a friend, who believes in me would teach me to believe in myself.

A friend turned angel. Maybe I need to tell her she is the angel in my life. Even angels need support and validation.

I visualized our conversation. It would go something like this:

Me: "Nance, how many years have we been friends?"

Nancy: "About forty."

Me: "Ya, that sounds about right. I don't wear heels anymore."

Nancy: "I never wore heels."

Me: "I wear long pants to hide my varicose veins."

Nancy: "My legs are pure muscle now."

Me: "Ya sure. Do you remember when we first met?"

Nancy: "Sure, it was at a church in Chicago."

Me: "You were Brent's first Sunday school teacher. I remember I liked you right away."

Nancy: "I liked you too. In those days, you were a glamorous dresser."

Me: "What? Are you sure?"

Nancy: "All those purple outfits."

Me: "Did you notice my keen mind?"

Nancy: "No."

Me: "I want to tell you something. Thank you for being my friend. Thank you for being the angel in my life and believing in me."

Nancy: "It was a tough job but someone had to do it."

We would then laugh like we did forty years ago.

Jeanmarie Dwyer-Wrigley

Jeanmarie Dwyer-Wrigley, M.S., has been facilitating women's groups since 1979. Her achievements include co-founding "A Woman's Place", a drop-in center for homeless women in Chicago. She opened the doors of WomensWisdom in 1993. She was awarded the Marilyn Gorski Service from Loyola Mundelein University for work with homeless women and the Appreciation Service Award from the Naperville/Lisle Women's Association. She has appeared on cable television shows regarding self-esteem empowerment. She obtained a Master of Science degree, with a focus on addictions counseling. She is also a handwriting analyst. Her hobbies are reading, tap dancing, acting and her two cats, Tuffy and Nighty Nite. She lives with her husband in the northwest suburbs.

Jeanmarie Dwyer-Wrigley

WomensWisdom

The Dance Bldg. 1330 Webford

Des Plaines, IL 60016

847-258-7255

Cell 224-200-0273

wwwomenswisdom@aol.com

www.womenswisdom.org

OVERCOMING
Mediocrity ©

It's time to share YOUR Super Hero Story in our next Overcoming Mediocrity book!

www.DPWNPublishing.com

Download your FREE Story Creation Guide to get started

bit.ly/6stepg

Or buy it on Amazon amazon